Films Directed by Edgar Wright (Film Guide)

Table of Contents

A Fistful of Fingers 1
Dead Right (film) 1
Grindhouse (film) 3
Hot Fuzz 10
Scott Pilgrim vs. the World 15
Shaun of the Dead 20
The World's End 23

Preface

Each chapter in this book ends with a URL to a hyperlinked online version. Use the online version to access related pages, websites, footnotes, tables, color photos, updates, or to see the chapter's contributors. Click the edit link to suggest changes. Please type the URL exactly as it appears. If you change the URL's capitalization, for example, it may not work.

Purchase of this book entitles you to a free trial membership in the publisher's book club at www.booksllc.net. (Time limited offer.) Simply enter the barcode number from the back cover onto the membership form on our home page. The book club entitles you to select from millions of books at no additional charge, including a digital copy of this and related books to read on the go. Simply enter the title or subject onto the search form to find them.

If you have any questions, could you please be so kind as to consult our Frequently Asked Questions page at www.booksllc.net/faqs.cfm? You are also welcome to contact us there.

Publisher: Books LLC, Wiki Series, Memphis, TN, USA, 2012.

A Fistful of Fingers

A Fistful of Fingers	
Directed by	Edgar Wright
Produced by	Edgar Wright Daniel Figuero Zygi Kamasa Gareth Owen
Written by	Edgar Wright
Music by	François Evans
Cinematography	Alvin Leong
Editing by	Giles Harding
Distributed by	Blue Dolphin Film Distribution
Release date(s)	1994
Running time	78 minutes
Country	United Kingdom
Language	English

A Fistful of Fingers is a 1994 British film written and directed by Edgar Wright.

It is a homonymous remake of an earlier, and even lower-budget, movie by Wright and starring Graham Low which had been made while they were still at school. The original *Fistful of Fingers* was never picked up by a distributor, but did receive enough local attention - along with his other similarly spoof-based school-era work such as "Carbolic Soap", "The Unparkables" and "Rolf Harris Saves the World" - for Wright to win funding for the 1994 remake.

Cast

Graham Low as 'No-Name'
Oli van der Vijver as The Squint
Nicola Stapleton as Floozy
Martin Curtis as Running Sore
Jeremy Beadle as Himself
Neil Mullarkey as Stand Up Comedian
Dan Palmer as 'Pile-On' Kid
Mark Sheffield as Calamity Keith
Edgar Wright as Cheesy Voiceover Artist/Two Bit Farmer Cameo
Quentin Green as Jimmy James
Source http://en.wikipedia.org/wiki/A_Fistful_of_Fingers

Dead Right (film)

Dead Right	
Directed by	Edgar Wright
Produced by	Edgar Wright
Written by	Edgar Wright
Starring	Edward Scotland Martin Curtis Richard Green Amy Bowles
Music by	Edgar Wright
Cinematography	Edgar Wright
Editing by	Edgar Wright
Distributed by	Edgar Wright
Release date(s)	1993
Running time	48 Minutes
Country	United Kingdom
Language	English
Budget	£275

Dead Right is an early short film from *Spaced* and *Shaun of the Dead* director Edgar Wright. Filmed in 1992 and 1993 in his hometown of Wells, England when Wright was only 18. He wrote, edited, produced and directed the film as well as shooting and recording the sound. It is a Zucker Brothers style comedy that parodies the action thriller genre, most notably the *Dirty Harry* series (*Dead Right* was the working title for the original *Dirty Harry*). The film is shot on SVHS and contains an impressive cast of 70 actors (mostly amateur), mainly made up of Wright's school friends and colleagues. Clips from the film were first broadcast on *Take Over TV* - the Channel 4 series consisting entirely of video clips sent in by viewers - that also launched the careers of comedy duo Adam and Joe.

Plot

The film opens with a parody of the Simon Bates intro that used to accompany VHS rentals where Bates would explain to the viewer what certificate the film had received - 18 apparently - and what adult content they could expect to see.

The story begins with a serial killer bumping off the residents of a small Somerset community. Maverick DI Barry Stern is assigned to the case and - despite his reluctance - is partnered with by-the-book fellow DI Mike Tight.

On their first time out together Barry shoots a dealer trying to sell him cocaine in a public toilet. Meanwhile the killer stalks a woman home from the supermarket and kills her by electrocution with a kitchen light.

Mike and Barry show up at the scene of the crime and discover the woman bludgeoned to death. A box of cereal has been left on her head leading Barry to summise that they are now looking for a cereal killer.

Back at the precinct Mike addresses his fellow inspectors. He tells them that in order to catch the killer they must look at and obey the formula that most cop movies go by even though it is a British movie and there won't be any car chases. Barry points out that the partner usually dies in these kind of movies but Mike says he is thinking more along the lines of the *Lethal Weapon* films.

The following day the police stakeout the local supermarket where they expect the killer to strike next. Barry is disguised as a mime. Mike is disguised an old lady in order to ensnare the killer. A small boy asks Barry for a mime. Barry gives him the finger that leads to him getting beaten up by the boy's elder brother.

Meanwhile Mike proceeds to the local park followed by the killer. Once there he realizes he is being followed and radios for help but it's too late. The killer attacks Mike and stabs him. Barry arrives on bike to find Mike dying. Mike says he loves Barry and gets him to give him a final kiss. Before he dies he tells him to look in the script to see where the killer is hiding out.

Barry arrives at a creepy looking house. There he is captured by the killer and tied to a chair. Barry says he knows who he is and proceeds to tell him his back-story: The killer is Philip Quinn. As a child he was made to eat cereal every day. He couldn't do it and in later years developed an inferiority complex about it. He then murdered his parents with a Black and Decker jigsaw and inherited their estate. He surrounded himself with waifs-and-strays that, like him, were hooked on cereal and slowly built up an army of hockey stick carrying box-men. He got a job at the local supermarket to satisfy his desire for cereal but he couldn't stand it when people would buy it for themselves and so he would follow them home and murder them.

Philip leaves Barry under the watchful eye of his beautiful sister Antonia. She seduces him and ten seconds later they are lying in bed together post-coitus. Barry handcuffs her to the chair and makes his escape.

Outside Barry encounters one of the box-men. He manages to defeat him by jumping on his face, which blows up. Meanwhile Antonia sounds the alarm which summons a whole army of box-men. They chase him into a room that turns out to be an armoury. He tools-up and proceeds outside to face his adversaries. A gun battle ensues during which Barry discovers that one of the box-men is MI5 undercover agent Nigel Roscoe. The pair join forces to fend off the box-men. After a lengthy action sequence they manage to slaughter the army leading to much splatter and carnage. However by this point Antonia has escaped and she hurls a knife into Nigel's back killing him. Barry shoots Antonia in the head.

Back at the supermarket Philip is working. Barry turns up to catch him but DI Jackson is waiting there to take Barry in. Barry subdues Philip but when Jackson interferes Barry lets Philip go in order to recapture him elsewhere. He tells Jackson not to follow him and lays chase.

In the local park Philip takes Edgar the director hostage and kills him. Barry breaks character, grabs a passing extra and gets her to direct the rest of the film.

Barry corners Philip in a playground. The pair have a showdown where they fight it out one-on-one. The fight culminates with Barry shooting Philip in the chest but only after reciting the "do you feel lucky" speech from *Dirty Harry*. Philip begs for mercy and says he wants to be Barry's best friend. Barry shoots him in the head.

As the police show up to clear up the mess Barry has created he sits forlornly on a park bench. Disillusioned with the police he throws his badge away before riffling through his pockets and pulling out a pin, a police radio and a grenade. Realizing too late that the pin was from the grenade it goes off.

Cast

Edward Scotland as Barry Stern
Martin Curtis as Philip Quinn
Richard Green as Mike Tight
Oliver Evans as Jackson
Peter Wild as Chief
Gavin Elwood as Enfield Bow
Rob Yarde as Nigel Roscoe
Amy Bowles as Antonia Quinn
Graham Low as The Box Monster
Ian Hill as Dead Before Credits
David Scotland as Simon Bates
David Denning as Gateway Employee (Cameo)
Gregory Curtis as Young Philip Quinn
Daniel Rowlinson as The Ginger Kid
Quentin Green as vexed cop

Production

Director Edgar Wright had won a Super VHS camera from a competition on the Saturday morning kids TV show *Going Live!* and so was able to make his own amateur shorts. At the time of the film's production he was a student at the Arts Institute of Bournemouth and would only be able to shoot the film whilst back home during term breaks.

The shooting script was only a first draft and not properly formatted. The budget for the film came solely out of Wright's pocket and went mainly on tape stock, props (water pistols painted black), costumes and food colouring. The surprisingly large cast was made up of his friends but he has said he went "outside my social circle" when it came to filling all the roles the film had to offer.

Dead Right contains many early examples of filming techniques that would later become Wright's trademarks such as transitions, whip-pans, wipes, tracking steady-cam shots and dolly zooms.

However there are very few sound effects unlike his later films for example *Hot Fuzz* where there is a heavy reliance on sound.

Both *Dead Right* and *Hot Fuzz* were attempts to do a British cop movie in the style of a US cop movie.

Wright says "There was a little wave of sub-standard British thrillers I used to think were quite pathetic trying to take on the Americans at their own game and failing miserably. That was the germ of the idea . . . to have our cake and eat it by both examining the gulf between British action films and American ones and trying to become more American."

Source http://en.wikipedia.org/wiki/Dead_Right_(film)

Grindhouse (film)

Theatrical release poster

Grindhouse	
Directed by	Robert Rodriguez (*Terror, Machete*)
	Quentin Tarantino (*Proof*)
	Rob Zombie (*Werewolf Woman of the SS*)
	Edgar Wright (*Don...*)
	Eli Roth (*Thanksgiving*)
	Jason Eisener (*Hobo a Shotgun*)
Produced by	Elizabeth Avellan
	Erica Steinberg
	Robert Rodriguez
	Quentin Tarantino
Written by	Robert Rodriguez
	Quentin Tarantino
Starring	Rose McGowan
	Freddy Rodriguez
	Josh Brolin
	Marley Shelton
	Kurt Russell
	Rosario Dawson
	Mary Elizabeth Winstead
	Zoë Bell
	Vanessa Ferlito
	Naveen Andrews
	Fergie
	Bruce Willis
Music by	Robert Rodriguez
	Graeme Revell (*PT*)
Cinematography	Robert Rodriguez
	Quentin Tarantino
Editing by	Robert Rodriguez
	Sally Menke (*DP*)
Studio	Troublemaker Studios
	The Weinstein Company
Distributed by	Dimension Films
	Vivendi Entertainment
Release date(s)	April 6, 2007
Running time	191 minutes
Country	United States
Language	English
	Spanish
Budget	$53 million
Box office	$25,422,088

Grindhouse is a 2007 action-horror/exploitation double feature co-written, produced, and directed by Robert Rodriguez and Quentin Tarantino. The double feature consists of two feature-length segments, Rodriguez's *Planet Terror* and Tarantino's *Death Proof*, and is bookended by fictional trailers for upcoming attractions, advertisements, and in-theater announcements. The film's title derives from the U.S. film industry term "grindhouse", which refers to (now mostly defunct) movie theaters specializing in B movies, often exploitation films, shown in a multiple-feature format. The film's ensemble cast includes Rose McGowan, Freddy Rodriguez, Michael Biehn, Jeff Fahey, Josh Brolin, Marley Shelton, Naveen Andrews, Fergie, Bruce Willis, Kurt Russell, Rosario Dawson, Tracie Thoms, Mary Elizabeth Winstead and stuntwoman Zoë Bell.

Rodriguez's segment, *Planet Terror*, revolves around an outfit of rebels attempting to survive an onslaught of zombie-like creatures as they feud with a rogue military unit, while Tarantino's segment, *Death Proof*, focuses on a misogynistic, psychopathic stunt man who targets young women, murdering them with his "death proof" stunt car. Each feature is preceded by faux trailers of exploitation films in other genres that were developed by other directors.

After the film was released on April 6, 2007, ticket sales performed significantly below box office analysts' expectations despite mostly positive critic reviews. In much of the rest of the world, each feature was released separately in extended versions. Two soundtracks were also released for the features and include music and audio snippets from the film. This film later found more success on DVD and Blu-ray. In several interviews, despite the box office failure, the directors have expressed their interest in a possible sequel to the film due its critical acclaim and successful home media sales. The series has three spin-offs based on its fake trailers: *Machete*, *Hobo with a Shotgun*, and *Machete Kills*.

Planet Terror

In a rural town in Texas, go-go dancer Cherry Darling decides to quit her low-paying job and find another use for her numerous "useless" talents. She runs into mysterious ex-boyfriend El Wray at the Bone Shack, a restaurant owned by J.T. Hague. Meanwhile, a group of military officials, led by the demented Lt. Muldoon, are making a business transaction with a scientist named Abby for mass quantities of a deadly biochemical agent known as DC2 (codename "Project Terror"). Muldoon learns that Abby has an extra supply on hand and attempts to take him hostage. Abby intentionally releases the gas into the air. The gas reaches the town and turns its residents into deformed bloodthirsty, man-eating psychopaths, mockingly referred to as "sickos" by the surviving humans. The infected townspeople are treated by the sinister Dr. William Block and his abused, neglected anesthesiologist wife Dakota at a local hospital. As the patients quickly become enraged aggressors, Cherry and El Wray lead a team of accidental warriors into the night, struggling to find safety.

Cast

Rose McGowan as Cherry Darling- A GoGo Dancer. After Cherry's leg is torn off by sickos, she is given a special prosthetic leg in the form of a high powered machine gun.
Freddy Rodriguez as El Wray- The Ex boyfriend of Cherry Darling. The two meet and take on the sickos together which causes them to fall in love again.
Josh Brolin as Dr. William Block- The husband of Dr. Dakota Block, the father of Tony Block and the son-in-law of Sherif Earl McGraw. He tries to kill Dakota because she cheated on him with Tammy.
Marley Shelton as Dr. Dakota Block- The estranged daughter of Sherif Earl McGraw. Dakota is also the wife of Dr. William Block, with whom she shares a son, Tony Block.
Jeff Fahey as J.T. Hague- The owner and head chef of the Bone Shack, and is known for having the best BBQ recipes in the world. He's Sheriff Hauge's brother.
Michael Biehn as Sheriff Hague- J.T.'s brother hates El Wray but later likes him because El Wray saves his life.
Bruce Willis as Lt. Muldoon- A scientist who caused the sickos. He has the gas to protect himself from the deadly poison which everyone in the movie wants.
Naveen Andrews as Dr. John "Abby" Abbington- A scientist and possible terrorist. He has the cure for the disease that turned everyone into sickos.
Rebel Rodriguez as Tony Block- The son of Dr. Dakota Block and Dr. William Block.
Michael Parks as Earl McGraw- The estranged father of Dr. Dakota Block.
Nicky Katt as Joe- Get's bitten by the sickos and later on becomes one.
Stacy Ferguson as Tammy Visan- The girl Dr. Dakota Block is having an affair with.
Quentin Tarantino as Lewis (Rapist #1)- A rapist who tries to rape Cherry and Dr. Dakota Block.
Tom Savini as Deputy Tolo- Get's his finger bitten off by the sickos then gets eaten alive by them.

Death Proof

Three friends – Arlene, Shanna, and radio disc jockey "Jungle" Julia Lucai – spend a night in Austin, Texas celebrating Julia's birthday, unknowingly followed by a mysterious man in a souped-up 1971 Chevy Nova. The man, Stuntman Mike, stalks the young women with his "death proof car", eventually killing all three. Fourteen months later, Stuntman Mike, now in Tennessee and driving a 1969 Dodge Charger, tails another group of young women – Lee, Abernathy, Kim, and stuntwoman Zoë – a group of women working below the line in Hollywood, whose Stock 1970 Dodge Challenger proves a worthy adversary.

Cast

Kurt Russell as Stuntman Mike- Little is known about Stuntman Mike, except that he hangs around the Texas Chili Parlor and may or may not be a professional stuntman on various TV shows during the 1960s and 1970s.
Rosario Dawson as Abernathy- She is friends with Kim, Zoe, and Lee. She is a make-up artist for Lindsay Lohan.
Vanessa Ferlito as Arlene "Butterfly"- She is friends with Jungle Julia, Shanna, and Marcy visiting from New York. Stuntman Mike has been following her throughout the day.
Jordan Ladd as Shanna- She is friends with Jungle Julia, Arleane, and Marcy.
Rose McGowan as Pam- In the bar she needs a ride home and Stuntman Mike volunteers to take her. She eventually becomes the first victim in Death Proof
Sydney Tamiia Poitier as "Jungle" Julia Lucai- A popular radio DJ in Austin, Texas. She went to school with Pam where she bullied her and slept around a lot.
Zoë Bell as Zoë- Friends with Abernathy, Kim and Lee. She straps herself to a car while Kim is driving very fast and Abernathy is in the passenger seat where Stuntman Mike is ready to attack.
Tracie Thoms as Kim- She is friends with Abernathy, Zoe, and Lee. She is a professional stuntwoman.
Mary Elizabeth Winstead as Lee Montgomery- She is friends with Abernathy, Zoe and Kim. She is a young actress while shooting a cheerleader movie in Tennessee.
Quentin Tarantino as Warren- The owner and bartender of the Texas Chili Parlor.
Michael Parks as Earl McGraw- Sheriff who works on Stuntman Mike's case.
James Parks as Edgar Mcgraw- The son of the sheriff who also works on Stuntman Mike's case along with his father.
Nicky Katt as Counter Guy- Sells Abernathy a magazine and tries to hit on her.
Marley Shelton as Dr. Dakota Block- The doctor to Stuntman Mike

Fictitious trailers

Before each segment, there are trailers advertising fake films, as well as vintage theater snipes and an ad for a fictional restaurant called Acuña Boys. According to Rodriguez, it was Tarantino's idea to film fake trailers for *Grindhouse*. "I didn't even know about it until I read it in the trades. It said something like 'Rodriguez and Tarantino doing a double feature and Tarantino says

Eli Roth directs the fictitous trailer *Thanksgiving*.

there's gonna be fake trailers.' And I thought, 'There are?'" Rodriguez and Tarantino had originally planned to make all of the film's fake trailers themselves. According to Rodriguez, "We had so many ideas for trailers. I made *Machete*. I shot lobby cards and the poster and cut the trailer and sent it to Quentin, and he just flipped out because it looked so vintage and so real. He started showing it around to Eli Roth and to Edgar Wright, and they said, 'Can we do a trailer? We have an idea for a trailer!' We were like, 'Hey, let them shoot it. If we don't get around to shooting ours, we'll put theirs in the movie. If theirs come out really great, we'll put it in the movie to have some variety.' Then Rob Zombie came up to me in October at the Scream Awards and said, 'I have a trailer: *Werewolf Women of the SS*.' I said, 'Say no more. Go shoot it. You got me.'" Each trailer was shot in two days. While Wright and Roth shot only what ended up on screen, Zombie shot enough footage to work into a half-hour film and was particularly pained to edit it down. Some Canadian screening releases included the South by Southwest-winning trailer *Hobo with a Shotgun*.

Machete

Rodriguez wrote *Machete* in 1993 as a full feature for Danny Trejo. "I had cast him in *Desperado* and I remember thinking, 'Wow, this guy should have his own series of Mexploitation movies like Charles Bronson or like Jean-Claude Van Damme.' So I wrote him this idea of a federale from Mexico who gets hired to do hatchet jobs in the U.S. I had heard sometimes FBI or DEA have a really tough job that they don't want to get their own agents killed on, they'll hire an agent from Mexico to come do the job for $25,000. I thought, 'That's Machete. He would come and do a really dangerous job for a lot of money to him but for everyone else over here it's peanuts.' But I never got around to making it." The trailer was made into a feature film which was released in September 2010, with two sequels to follow.

Werewolf Women of the SS

Rob Zombie's contribution, *Werewolf Women of the SS*, stared Nicolas Cage as Fu Manchu; Udo Kier as Franz Hess, the commandant of Death Camp 13; Zombie's wife, Sheri; and Sybil Danning as SS officers/sisters Eva and Gretchen Krupp (The She-Devils of Belzac). Professional wrestlers Andrew "Test" Martin and Oleg Prudius (better known as Vladimir Kozlov) also featured, plus Olja Hrustic, Meriah Nelson, and Lorielle New as the Werewolf Women. According to Zombie, "Basically, I had two ideas. It was either going to be a Nazi movie or a women-in-prison film, and I went with the Nazis. There're all those movies like *Ilsa, She Wolf of the SS*; *Fräulein Devil*; and *Love Camp 7*—I've always found that to be the most bizarre genre." Zombie is also quoted as saying "I was getting very conceptual in my own mind with it. [...] A lot of times these movies would be made like, 'Well, you know, I've got a whole bunch of Nazi uniforms, but I got this Chinese set too. We'll put 'em together!' They start jamming things in there, so I took that approach."

Don't

Edgar Wright's contribution, *Don't*, was produced in the style of a 1970s' Hammer House of Horror film trailer. The trailer featured appearances from Jason Isaacs, Matthew Macfadyen, singer Katie Melua, Lee Ingleby, Georgina Chapman, Emily Booth, Stuart Wilson, Lucy Punch, Rafe Spall, Wright regulars Simon Pegg and Nick Frost, and a voice-over by Will Arnett. Mark Gatiss, MyAnna Buring, Peter Serafinowicz, Michael Smiley and Nicola Cunningham (who played the zombie "Mary" in *Shaun of the Dead*), among others, made cameo appearances though they eventually went uncredited. To get the necessary 1970s' look, Wright used vintage lenses and old-style graphics. During editing, he scratched some of the film with steel wool and dragged it around a parking lot to make it appear neglected by wayward projectionists. According to Wright, "In the '70s, when American International would release European horror films, they'd give them snazzier titles. And the one that inspired me was this Jorge Grau film: In the UK, it's called *The Living Dead at Manchester Morgue*. In Spain and in Italy, I think it's called *Do Not Speak Ill of the Dead*. But in the States, it was called *Don't Open the Window*. I just loved the fact that there isn't a big window scene in the film—it's all based around the spin and the voiceover not really telling you what the hell is going on in the film." On the Charlie Rose talk show, Quentin Tarantino also pointed out another aspect of American advertising of British films in the 1970s that is being referenced—none of the actors have any dialogue in the trailer, as if the trailer was intentionally edited to prevent American viewers from realizing that the film is British.

Thanksgiving

Eli Roth's contribution is a promo for the slasher opus *Thanksgiving*. Produced in the style of holiday-based slasher films such as *Halloween*, *Black Christmas*, *April Fool's Day* and *My Bloody Valentine*, the trailer starred Jeff Rendell as a killer who stalks victims dressed as a pilgrim; Jordan Ladd, Jay Hernandez, and Roth himself as his intended victims; and Michael Biehn as the Sheriff. The design for the titles in *Thanksgiving* was based on a *Mad* magazine slasher parody titled *Arbor Day*. Select excerpts of the score from *Creepshow* were used.

According to Roth, "My friend Jeff, who plays the killer pilgrim – we grew up in Massachusetts, we were huge slasher movie fans and every November we were waiting for the Thanksgiving slasher movie. We had the whole movie worked out: A kid who's in love with a turkey, and then his father killed it, and then he killed his family and went away to a mental institution and came back and took revenge on the town. I called Jeff and said, 'Dude, guess what, we don't have to make the movie, we can just shoot the best parts.'" "Shooting the trailer was so much fun," Roth has stated, "because every shot is a money shot. Every shot is decapitation or nudity. It's so ridiculous, it's absurd. It's just so wrong and sick that it's right."

Roth's fake trailer contained elements that almost earned *Grindhouse* an NC-17 rating, including a cheerleader simultaneously stripping, bouncing on a trampoline and getting stabbed in the vulva, and three decapitations, one of which occurring as the victim's girlfriend performs fellatio on him. According to Roth, "Instead of seeing it spread out in a feature, watching it all jammed together nonstop makes it more shocking. But we had a great discussion with the ratings board. They got it. Once they saw it with all the bad splices and the distress and scratches they were fine with it." Roth confirmed in an interview with Cinema Blend's Eric Eisenberg that he and co-writer Jeff Rendell are working on a possible feature film.

Hobo with a Shotgun

Some screenings of *Grindhouse* (mainly in Canada) also featured a fake trailer for a film titled *Hobo with a Shotgun*. The trailer, created by Dartmouth, Nova Scotia filmmakers Jason Eisener, John Davies, and Rob Cotterill, won Robert Rodriguez's South by Southwest *Grindhouse* trailers contest. In the trailer, David Brunt plays a vagabond with a 20-gauge shotgun (changed to a 12-gauge for the actual movie) who becomes a vigilante. In the trailer, he is shown killing numerous persons, ranging from armed robbers to corrupt cops to a pedophilic Santa Claus. The trailer was available in certain selected movie theaters in the United States and Canada.

In 2010, the trailer was made into a full-length feature film starring Rutger Hauer as the hobo, with David Brunt playing a dirty cop. *Hobo With a Shotgun* was the second of *Grindhouse*'s fake trailers to be turned into a feature film, the first being *Machete*. The release date for *Hobo* was March 25, 2011 for Canada, release on April 1, 2011 for American Video On Demand and theatrically released on May 6, 2011 for USA.

History and development

The poster for a double feature consisting of the films *Dragstrip Girl* and *Rock All Night* sparked the idea for *Grindhouse*.

The idea for *Grindhouse* came to Robert Rodriguez and Quentin Tarantino when Tarantino set up screenings of double features in his house, complete with trailers before and in between the films. During one screening in 2003, Rodriguez noticed that he owned the same double feature movie poster as Tarantino for the 1957 films *Dragstrip Girl* and *Rock All Night*. Rodriguez asked Tarantino, "I always wanted to do a double feature. Hey, why don't you direct one and I'll do the other?" Tarantino quickly replied, "And we've got to call it *Grindhouse*!"

The film's name originates from the American term for theaters that played "all the exploitation genres: kung fu, horror, Giallo, sexploitation, the 'good old boy' redneck car-chase movies, blaxploitation, spaghetti Westerns—all those risible genres that were released in the 70s." According to Rodriguez, "The posters were much better than the movies, but we're actually making something that lives up to the posters."

Rodriguez first came up with the idea for *Planet Terror* during the production of *The Faculty*: "I remember telling Elijah Wood and Josh Hartnett, all these young actors, that zombie movies were dead and hadn't been around in a while, but that I thought they were going to come back in a big way because they'd been gone for so long. I said, 'We've got to be there first.' I had [a script] I'd started writing. It was about 30 pages, and I said to them, 'There are characters for all of you to play.' We got all excited about it, and then I didn't know where to go with it. The introduction was about as far as I'd gotten, and then I got onto other movies. Sure enough, the zombie [movie] invasion happened and they all came back again, and I was like, 'Ah, I knew that I should've made my zombie film.'" The story was reapproached when Tarantino and Rodriguez developed the idea for *Grindhouse*.

As *Planet Terror* took shape, Tarantino developed the story for *Death Proof*, based on his fascination for the way stuntmen would "death-proof" their cars. As long as they were driving, stuntmen could slam their cars headfirst into a brick wall at 60 mph (97 km/h) and survive. This inspired Tarantino to create a slasher film featuring a deranged stuntman who stalks and murders sexy young women with his "death-proof" car. Tarantino remembers, "I realized I couldn't do a straight slasher film, because with the exception of women-in-prison films, there is no other genre quite as rigid. And if you break that up, you aren't really doing it anymore. It's inorganic, so I realized— let me take the structure of a slasher film and just do what I do. My version is going to be fucked up and disjointed, but it seemingly uses the structure of a slasher film, hopefully against you."

According to Rodriguez, "[Tarantino] had an idea and a complete vision for it right away when he first talked about it. He started to tell me the story and said, 'It's got this death-proof car in it.' I said, 'You have to call it *Death Proof.*' I helped title the movie, but that's it." Of the car chases, Tarantino stated, "CGI for car stunts doesn't make any sense to me—how is that supposed to be impressive? [...] I don't think there have been any good car chases since I started making films in '92—to me, the last terrific car chase was in *Terminator 2*. And *Final Destination 2* had a magnificent car action piece. In between that, not a lot. Every time a stunt happens, there's twelve cameras and they use every angle for Avid editing, but I don't feel it in my stomach. It's just action."

Production

Direction

According to actress Marley Shelton, "Rodriguez and Tarantino really co-directed, at least *Planet Terror*. Quentin was on set a lot. He had notes and adjustments to our performances and he changed lines every once in a while. Of course, he always deferred to Robert on *Planet Terror* and vice versa for *Death Proof*. So it's really both of their brainchild." Tarantino has stated, "I can't imagine doing *Grindhouse* with any other director in the way me and Robert did it because I just had complete faith and trust in him. So much so that we didn't actually see each other's movie completed until three weeks before the film opened. It was as if we worked in little vacuums and cut our movies down, and then put them together and watched it all play, and then made a couple of little changes after that, and pretty much that was it."

Casting

Many of the cast members had previously worked with both directors. Before appearing in *Grindhouse*, Marley Shelton had auditioned for *The Faculty*, but Rodriguez chose not to cast her. She was eventually cast in the role of a customer in the opening sequence of *Sin City*. Bruce Willis had appeared in both Tarantino's *Pulp Fiction* and Rodriguez's *Sin City*, in addition to having a cameo appearance in a segment Tarantino directed for the anthology film *Four Rooms*. Tom Savini had previously acted in *From Dusk Till Dawn*, which was written by Tarantino and directed by Rodriguez. Michael Parks reprises the role of Earl McGraw in *Planet Terror* and *Death Proof*. Parks first portrayed the role in *From Dusk Till Dawn*. His son, James, appears in *Death Proof* as Edgar McGraw, a character that first appeared in *From Dusk Till Dawn 2: Texas Blood Money*. The first time the two characters appeared together was in Tarantino's *Kill Bill*. Tarantino himself plays small roles in both segments of *Grindhouse*, and director Eli Roth, who contributed the fake trailer *Thanksgiving* and whose film *Hostel* was produced by Tarantino, has a cameo in *Death Proof*.

Tarantino attempted to cast both Kal Penn and Sylvester Stallone in *Death Proof*, but both were unable to work due to prior commitments. In an interview, Tarantino revealed that he decided to cast Kurt Russell as the killer stunt driver because "for people of my generation, he's a true hero...but now, there's a whole audience out there that doesn't know what Kurt Russell can do. When I open the newspaper and see an ad that says 'Kurt Russell in *Dreamer*,' or 'Kurt Russell in *Miracle*,' I'm not disparaging these movies, but I'm thinking: When is Kurt Russell going to be a badass again?"

Cinematography

Rodriguez and Tarantino each acted as cinematographer on their segments. Although Rodriguez had previously worked as the cinematographer on six of his own feature films, *Death Proof* marked Tarantino's first credit as a cinematographer. The director of photography for Rob Zombie's fake trailer *Werewolf Women of the SS* was Phil Parmet, whom Zombie had first worked with on *The Devil's Rejects*. The director of photography for Eli Roth's fake trailer *Thanksgiving* was Milan Chadima, whom Roth had previously worked with on *Hostel*.

Special effects

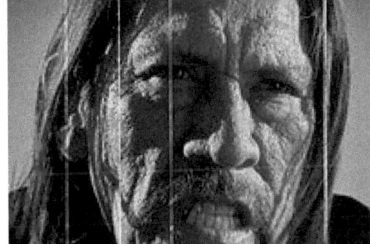

The intentionally "aged" look of the film, as seen in the trailer *Machete*.

Though set in modern day, film uses various unconventional techniques to make the films look like those that were shown in grindhouse theaters in the 1970s. Throughout both feature-length segments and the fake trailers, the film is intentionally damaged to make it look like many of the exploitation films of the 1970s, which were generally shipped around from theater to theater and usually ended up in bad shape. To reproduce the look of damaged film reels in *Planet Terror*, five of the six 25,000-frame reels were edited with real film damage, plug-ins, and stock footage.

Planet Terror makes heavy use of digital effects throughout the film. Perhaps the most notable effect is Cherry's (Rose McGowan) fake leg. To accomplish the fake leg that Cherry sports after her accident, during post-production the effects teams digitally removed McGowan's right leg from the shots and replaced it with computer-generated props—first a table leg and then an M16 rifle. During shooting for these scenes, McGowan wore a special cast which restricted her leg movement to give her the correct motion, and helped the effects artists to digitally remove it during post-production.

Editing

During editing, Tarantino and Rodriguez came up with the idea of inserting "missing reels" into the film. "[Quentin] was about to show an Italian crime movie with Oliver Reed," Rodriguez recalls, "and he was saying, 'Oh, it's got a missing reel in it. But it's really interesting because after the missing reel, you don't know if he slept with a girl or he didn't because she says he did and he says that he didn't. It leaves you guessing, and the movie still works with 20 minutes gone out of it.' I thought, 'Oh, my God, that's what we've got to do. We've got to have a missing reel!' I'm going to use it in a way where it actually says 'missing reel' for 10 seconds, and then when we come back, you're arriving in the third act. [...] The late second acts in movies are usually the most predictable and the most boring, that's where the good guy really turns out to be the bad guy, and the bad guy is really good, and the couple becomes friends. Suddenly, though, in the third act, all bets are off and it's a whole new story anyway."

On the editing of *Death Proof*, Tarantino stated "There is half-an-hour's difference between my *Death Proof* and what is playing in *Grindhouse*. [...] I was like a brutish American exploitation distributor who cut the movie down almost to the point of incoherence. I cut it down to the bone and took all the fat off it to see if it could still exist, and it worked." An extended, 127-minute version of *Death Proof* was screened in competition for the Palme d'Or at the 60th Cannes Film Festival. Tarantino is quoted as saying "It works great as a double feature, but I'm just as excited if not more excited about actually having the world see *Death Proof* unfiltered. [...] It will be the first time everyone sees *Death Proof* by itself, including me."

Grindhouse is rated R in the United States for "strong graphic bloody violence and gore, pervasive language, some sexuality, nudity, and drug use". On March 15, 2007, *The New York Post* reported that the film would possibly require heavy and extensive cuts in order to avoid an NC-17 rating. Shortly after, the film officially received an R-rating from the MPAA. Ain't It Cool News reported that according to Tarantino, on-

ly minimal cuts were made which ended up totaling 20 seconds.

Soundtrack influences

The music for *Planet Terror* was composed by Rodriguez. Inspiration for his score came from John Carpenter, whose music was often played on set. A cover version of The Dead Kennedys' "Too Drunk to Fuck" performed by Nouvelle Vague was also featured. The soundtrack for *Death Proof* consists entirely of non-original music, including excerpts from the scores of other films. Soundtrack albums for both segments were released on April 3, 2007.

Response

Critical reception

Grindhouse was embraced favorably by the consensus of critics; review aggregator website Rotten Tomatoes reported that 83% of critics gave the film a positive review based on a sample of 185 reviews, with an average score of 7.3/10. At the website Metacritic, which utilizes a normalized rating system, the film earned a favorable rating of 77/100 based on 33 reviews by mainstream critics.

Entertainment Weekly awarded the film a "B+" rating, praising it as a "crazily funny and exciting tribute to the grimy glory days of 1970s exploitation films" that "will leave you laughing, gasping, thrilled at a movie that knows, at long last, how to put the bad back in badass." Peter Travers of *Rolling Stone* gave the film a positive review, commenting that "by stooping low without selling out, this babes-and-bullets tour de force gets you high on movies again." Critic James Berardinelli also enjoyed the film but was not as positive as other critics. Awarding the film three stars (out of four), Berardinelli found the film to be "cinema as an expression of pulp with attitude... [Rodriguez and Tarantino] are speaking from the hearts... but that doesn't mean everyone sitting in the theater will get it."

The critics who did not like the film were not amused by the film's graphic and comical violence, with Larry Ratliff of *San Antonio Express-News* noting that "this ambitious, scratched and weathered venture never manages a real death grip on the senses." Mick LaSalle of the *San Francisco Chronicle* awarded the film a high rating, but noted that "the Rodriguez segment is terrific; the Tarantino one long-winded and juvenile." Others, by contrast, have considered *Death Proof* to be a deeper and more noteworthy segment. Critic A. O. Scott of *The New York Times* notes that "[a]t a certain point in *Death Proof* the scratches and bad splices disappear, and you find yourself watching not an arch, clever pastiche of old movies and movie theaters but an actual movie." *Chicago Sun-Times* critic Roger Ebert was divided. He gave *Grindhouse* as a whole two and a half stars out of four, awarding *Planet Terror* two stars and *Death Proof* three stars. Ebert also noted the irony of "Grindhouse" largely being superseded by many big-budget R-rated mainstream films that included a great deal of nudity and graphic violence.

Critics generally enjoyed the fake trailers. Geoff Pevere of the *Toronto Star* wrote that the use of the trailers helps the film establish "... its credibility as both mock-artifact and geeky fetish object even before the opening feature." Todd McCarthy of *Variety* claimed that the trailers were "... excellent candidates for exploitation immortality." Jeff Vice of *Deseret News*, who gave the feature films negative reviews, called the trailers "... the strongest aspect of the entire presentation." Maitland McDonagh of *TV Guide* claimed "With the exception of *Werewolf Women*, which tries a little too hard, they're all spot-on pastiches."

The double feature appeared at number six on Jack Mathews and Owen Gleiberman's respective top ten lists for *New York Daily News* and *Entertainment Weekly*, and at number seven on Stephanie Zacharek's list for *Salon*. Marc Savlov listed *Death Proof* at number ten on his list for *The Austin Chronicle*.

Box office

Grindhouse did not perform well at the box office, surprising box office analysts and fans alike given the strong reviews and favorable media buzz. Costing $53 million to produce, *Grindhouse* opened poorly with "a disappointing $11.5 million" in the United States, making a per-theater average of $4,417; box office analysts originally predicted an opening weekend total of at least $20–$30 million.

The opening weekend box office total stood below not only the second weekends of *Blades of Glory* and *Meet the Robinsons*, but also fell below the opening weekend gross of the widely panned *Are We Done Yet?*. In an attempt to explain the film's disappointing opening weekend, box office analyst Brandon Gray suggested that *Grindhouse* "suffered the usual horror comedy dilemma that afflicted *Snakes on a Plane* and *Slither* among others: too funny to be scary, too scary to be funny." Box office analyst Lee Tistaert of popular tracking website Lee's Movie Info compared the result with what may have happened if Tarantino's *Kill Bill* saga had been released as one film, instead of two separate volumes. "Is it possible that Tarantino got his wish this time as a result of two back-to-back $60 million grosses?" he asked. Others attributed the film's disappointing opening to the timing of Easter weekend, noting that the weekend is more tailored for family-oriented films or light-comedy, not exploitative horror films. Quentin Tarantino is quoted as saying about the film's box office results, "It was disappointing, yeah. But the movie worked with the audience. [...] People who saw it loved it and applauded. [...] I'm proud of my flop." Harvey Weinstein said that he was so "incredibly disappointed" with the film's opening weekend that he was considering re-releasing it as two separate films and possibly adding back the "missing" scenes. The film has altogether earned $25,422,088 in ticket sales. Grindhouse was separated and released internationally. "Grindhouse: Death Proof" grossed $30,663,961. "Grindhouse: Planet Terror" grossed $10,871,224. This brought Grindhouse's total gross to $67,000,000.

Release

Theatrical

Outside the US and Canada, *Planet Terror* and *Death Proof* were released separately in extended versions, approximately two months apart. The poster artwork for each film's release in the Netherlands claimed that *Death Proof* would feature "coming attractions" from Rodriguez, while *Planet Terror* would feature "coming attractions" from Tarantino. While the separated version of *Planet Terror* includes the *Machete* trailer, none of the other fake trailers were included when the features were released individually.

In reaction to the possibility of a split in a foreign release, Tarantino stated "Especially if they were dealing with non-English language countries, they don't really have this tradition ... not only do they not really know what a grind house is, they don't even have the double feature tradition. So you are kind of trying to teach us something else." Many European fans saw the split as an attempt to increase profits by forcing audiences to pay twice for what was shown as a single film in the United States.

In the United Kingdom, *Death Proof* was released on September 21, 2007. The release of *Planet Terror* followed on November 9 with an eventual, theatrical, limited run of the entire Grindhouse feature the following year. *Death Proof* was screened in Europe in the extended version that was presented in competition at the Cannes film festival. The additional material includes scenes that were replaced in the American theatrical release version with a "missing reel" title card, such as the lap dance scene. A total of about 27 minutes were added for this version. In Australia, the edited version of *Death Proof* was first screened on November 1, 2007 as a separate film. However, from January 17, 2008, *Grindhouse* had limited screenings. In April 2008, *Grindhouse* was screened by Dendy Cinemas in one venue at a time across the country, through the use of a traveling 35 mm reel. In South America, *Planet Terror* was released on January 2010, while *Death Proof* was released on July 2010 at least in Brazil.

Home media

Star Michael Biehn signing a copy of the box set during an August 23, 2012 appearance at Midtown Comics in Manhattan.

Death Proof and *Planet Terror* were released separately on DVD in the United States. The trailers were omitted from *Death Proof*, with the exception of *Machete* which was from *Planet Terror*. *Death Proof* was released on September 18, 2007, with *Planet Terror* following on October 16, 2007. Both were two-disc special editions featuring extended versions of the films. Robert Rodriguez stated in his 10-Minute Film School that a box set of the two films would be available soon, and that his 10-Minute Cook School would appear on it. This release would also reportedly include *Hobo with a Shotgun*. A six-DVD edition of the film was released on March 21, 2008 in Japan, featuring the films in both their individual extended versions and in the abridged double feature presentation along with previously-unreleased special features.

Planet Terror and *Death Proof* were released individually on Blu-ray Disc on December 16, 2008 in North America. The Blu-ray edition of *Planet Terror* also contained a "scratch-free" version of the film that removed much of the damage effects, while the Blu-ray edition of *Death Proof* only contained the "damaged" version of the film. The theatrical version of *Grindhouse* was released on Region 2 DVD and the stand alone version of *Death Proof* HD DVD was released in Germany on December

31, 2009.

A two-disc Blu-ray "Special Edition" of *Grindhouse* was released on October 5, 2010 in the US by Vivendi Entertainment and has exclusive bonus features. This release marks the first time that US viewers can view the full *Grindhouse* "Double Feature Presentation" experience at home as it was originally released in theaters. The first disc of the 2-disc set contains *Death Proof* and *Planet Terror*, along with the faux trailers, including the "trailer" for *Machete*. The theatrical cut was released on DVD in Canada from Alliance Atlantis. All of the extras from the previous individual DVD releases were included, however none of the extras from the Special Edition Blu-ray were included.

Bill Moseley stated at FanExpo on August 27, 2010 that the Blu-ray would also include a 5-minute version of *Werewolf Women of the SS*.

Adaptations of fake trailers

In 2010, Rodriguez wrote and co-directed a feature-length adaptation of his fake trailer, *Machete*. All of the original actors from the trailer (save for the extras) returned to their posts for it. *Machete* turned out to be much more of a success at the box office than *Grindhouse*, grossing $44 million against a just-over $10 million budget. At the end of the film, the announcer says that there will be two sequels: *Machete Kills* and *Machete Kills Again*. Soon afterward, Rodriguez confirmed that the financing for the sequels was in place, and that once everyone was free, they could begin shooting.

The director of a trailer that played in some theaters in the United States and Canada (mainly the latter), *Hobo with a Shotgun*, Jason Eisener, also made a feature-length adaptation of it. Rutger Hauer replaced Dave Brunt as the titular character, though Brunt does make a cameo as a corrupt cop.

The adaptations received mainly positive reviews, with the general consensus being that they were cartoonishly enjoyable and gleefully violent homages to their reasons for being. Although *Hobo with a Shotgun* was not as big a box office success in the U.S. as it was in Canada, it has since gained a cult following there.

Recently, many of the other fake trailer directors have expressed interest in making their trailers into real films, including Edgar Wright and Eli Roth. Recently, Roth announced that he was making a different film, presumably meaning that the adaptation of *Thanksgiving* has been put on hold.

Sequel

Both Rodriguez and Tarantino have said that they are interested in making a sequel to *Grindhouse*. Tarantino said that he wants to shoot an "old-school Kung Fu movie in Mandarin with subtitles in some countries, and release a shorter, dubbed cut in others" for his segment. It has also been reported by Rotten Tomatoes that Edgar Wright may expand *Don't* into a feature film. According to Eli Roth, he and Wright have discussed the possibility of pairing *Don't* with *Thanksgiving* for a *Grindhouse* sequel. Roth is quoted as saying "We're talking to Dimension about it. I think they're still trying to figure out *Grindhouse 1* before we think about *Grindhouse 2*, but I've already been working on the outline for it and I would do it in a heartbeat."

Rodriguez announced plans to create a feature-length adaptation of the *Machete* trailer and release it by the time *Planet Terror* and *Death Proof* would be made available on DVD. However, due to various delays, the film was pushed back to a 2010 release date; *Machete* screened September 1 at the Venice Film Festival and was released across cinemas in the US on September 3, 2010.

Electra and Elise Avellan, Rodriguez's nieces who play the Crazy Babysitter Twins in both films, originally stated their uncle wanted to do a sequel featuring both *Machete* and *The Babysitter Twins*, but the latter concept did not materialize with the former's release. "Robert mentioned something about the end of the world and Hollywood action films, where we'd be trained in Mexico to come back here and fight," Electra Avellan told bloody-disgusting.com.

Source http://en.wikipedia.org/wiki/Grindhouse_(film)

Hot Fuzz

Hot Fuzz

International theatrical release poster

Directed by	Edgar Wright
Produced by	Nira Park Tim Bevan Eric Fellner
Written by	Edgar Wright Simon Pegg
Starring	Simon Pegg Nick Frost
Music by	David Arnold
Cinematography	Jess Hall
Editing by	Chris Dickens
Studio	StudioCanal Working Title Film Big Talk Production
Distributed by	Universal Pictures
Release date(s)	14 February 2007 (United Kingdom)
Running time	121 minutes
Country	United States United Kingdom France
Language	English
Budget	£8 million
Box office	$80,573,774

Hot Fuzz is a 2007 comedy film directed and co-written by Edgar Wright, and co-written and starring Simon Pegg alongside Nick Frost. The three had previously worked together on the television series *Spaced* and the 2004 film *Shaun of the Dead*. The film was directed by Wright and produced by Nira Park, and follows two police officers attempting to solve a series of mysterious deaths in a small English village.

Over a hundred action films were used as inspiration for developing the script, which Wright and Pegg worked on together. Filming took place over eleven weeks in early 2006, and featured an extensive cast along with various uncredited cameos. Visual effects were developed by ten artists to expand on or add explosive, gore, and gunfire scenes. Prior to the film's release it was promoted on video blogs during the production as well as at a San Diego Comic-Con panel.

Debuting on 14 February 2007 in the United Kingdom and 20 April in the United States, *Hot Fuzz* received wide acclaim with a 91% approval rating on Rotten Tomatoes and 81/100 from Metacritic. The total international box office gross reached $80,573,774 before its home media release. Shortly after the film's release, two different soundtracks were released in the UK and US. The film is the second in Wright and Pegg's planned *Three Flavours Cornetto Trilogy*, which also includes *Shaun of the Dead* and the upcoming *The World's End*.

Plot

Nicholas Angel (Simon Pegg), an extremely dedicated police officer in a London Police service, performs his duties so well that he is accused of making his colleagues look bad. As a result, his superiors transfer him to "crime-free" Sandford, a town in rural Gloucestershire. Once in Sandford, he immediately arrests a large group of under-age drinkers, and a drunk driver who turns out to be his partner, PC Danny Butterman (Nick Frost), the son of local police inspector Frank Butterman (Jim Broadbent). Danny, well-meaning but naive, is in awe of his new partner. Angel struggles to adjust to the slow, uneventful pace of the village. Despite clearing up several otherwise unnoticed crimes, including confiscating a naval mine and a number of unlicensed firearms, Angel soon finds his most pressing concern is an escaped swan. His attention to the letter of the law makes him the target of dislike and mockery by his co-workers. Angel and Butterman eventually bond over drinks at the local pub and action films such as *Point Break* and *Bad Boys II*.

A series of gruesome deaths shock the town; Angel investigates, believing them to be murders. He attempts to arrest Simon Skinner (Timothy Dalton), the manager of the local Somerfield supermarket, and member of Sandford's Neighbourhood Watch Alliance (NWA), under suspicion of murdering the victims due to their involvement in a lucrative property deal. Skinner is able to provide plausible explanations for all of Angel's charges, and a solid alibi.

Disappointed and concerned that he has become paranoid, Angel returns to his routine policing with Danny. However, he overhears a shopkeeper inquire about the 'killers'. He realizes that he was wrong in suspecting the murders to be the actions of one person. He takes his multiple-killer theory to Inspector Butterman, who asks him to sleep on it.

When Angel returns to his hotel room he is attacked by a cloaked figure. He knocks the attacker unconscious, discovering it's Michael Armstrong (Rory McCann), the trolley boy at Somerfield, sent by Skinner to kill Angel. Tipped off by Skinner on Michael's walkie-talkie, Angel heads to the nearby castle where he discovers the truth: Inspector Butterman and the NWA are obsessed with keeping Sandford's "Village of the Year" title, murdering anyone who they see as a threat to the village's image (even for frivolous reasons). The late Mrs Butterman had put everything into helping Sandford win the first "Village of the Year", but travellers ruined the park the night before the judges arrived, which drove her to committing suicide. While fleeing the mob, Angel discovers the bodies of various "problem" people whom the NWA had disposed of, but then Danny corners and stabs him.

Having tricked the NWA into believing that Angel is dead (having stabbed a packet of ketchup in Angel's notebook), Danny drives him to the village limits and releases him, insisting that he knew nothing about their true activities. Danny urges Angel to go back to London, reasoning that no one would believe the truth about Sandford. At a motorway service station, Angel sees *Point Break* and *Bad Boys II* on a nearby DVD rack and is inspired to stop the NWA. He drives back to town and arms himself with the guns he confiscated earlier, and with Danny's help engages the NWA in an increasingly destructive series of gun fights, taking down most of them non-fatally. After persuading their colleagues of the truth, Angel and Danny take the battle to Somerfield: Skinner and Inspector Butterman flee, and are pursued by Angel and Danny (who catch the swan en route) to the nearby model village. Angel fights Skinner one-on-one, until Skinner slips and impales his mouth on the spire of the miniature cathedral. Inspector Butterman attempts to escape in Angel's car, but crashes into a tree when the swan attacks him from the back seat.

Angel's former superiors arrive from London, begging him to return as the crime rate has risen without him, but Angel chooses to remain in Sandford. Back at the police station, Tom Weaver (Edward Woodward), the last remaining member of the NWA, attempts to shoot Angel with an antique blunderbuss, but Danny dives in front of Angel and takes the shot. As Weaver tries to reload, Angel kicks a rubbish bin in the chest of Weaver, causing him to fall into the confiscated naval mine, which then rolls over him, triggering it and destroying the station. Angel tears through the rubble, distraught as he uncovers an unresponsive Danny.

One year later, Inspector Angel lays flowers on a grave marked "Butterman"; it is revealed that Danny has survived and the grave is his mother's. Danny is now a sergeant and Angel the head of the Sandford Police Service, and the two head off to patrol Sandford.

Cast
Sandford Police Service
Simon Pegg as PC/Sgt./Insp. Nicholas Angel
Nick Frost as PC/Sgt. Danny Butterman
Jim Broadbent as Insp. Frank Butterman
Paddy Considine as DS Andy Wainwright
Rafe Spall as DC Andy Cartwright
Kevin Eldon as Sgt. Tony Fisher
Olivia Colman as PC Doris Thatcher
Karl Johnson as PC Bob Walker
Bill Bailey as the Sergeants Turner Sampson as Saxon

Neighbourhood Watch Alliance
Timothy Dalton as Simon Skinner
Edward Woodward OBE as Tom Weaver
Billie Whitelaw CBE as Joyce Cooper
Eric Mason as Bernard Cooper
Stuart Wilson as Dr. Robin Hatcher
Paul Freeman as Rev. Philip Shooter
Kenneth Cranham as James Reaper
Peter Wight as Roy Porter
Julia Deakin as Mary Porter
Patricia Franklin as Annette Roper
Lorraine Hilton as Amanda Paver
Tim Barlow as Mr. Treacher
Rory McCann as Michael Armstrong
Trevor Nicholis as Greg Prosser
Elizabeth Elvin as Sherri Prosser

Metropolitan Police Service
Martin Freeman as the Sergeant
Steve Coogan as the Inspector *(uncredited)*
Bill Nighy as the Ch. Insp. Kenneth
Cate Blanchett as Janine *(uncredited)*
Chris Waitt as Dave
Edgar Wright as Dave (Voice) *(uncredited)*
Joe Cornish as Bob
Robert Popper as "Not Janine"

Sandford residents
Stephen Merchant as Peter Ian Staker
Alice Lowe as Tina
David Bradley as Arthur Webley
Anne Reid as Leslie Tiller
Ben McKay as Peter Cocker
Adam Buxton as Tim Messenger
David Threlfall as Martin Blower
Lucy Punch as Eve Draper
Ron Cook as George Merchant
Edgar Wright as Shelf Stacker *(uncredited)*
Joseph McManners as Gabriel
Rory McCann as Michael Armstrong
Graham Low as The Living Statue
Alexander King as Aaron A Aaronson

While writing the script, the film's director and writer, Edgar Wright, as well as Simon Pegg, intended to include Nick Frost as the partner for Pegg's character. Frost revealed that he would do the film only if he could name his character, and he chose "Danny Butterman". Cast requirements included fifty people for speaking and non-speaking parts, and there were several casting calls for citizens of Wells, Somerset, to fill the roles, as the city was where most of the filming took place.

Cameos
British singer and actor Joseph McManners played a cameo role as a tearaway schoolboy, although his background story and an entire sub-plot surrounding his character were cut from the final version and can only be found within the DVD bonus features.

Wright revealed in an interview that Cate Blanchett was given her cameo role as Janine, Angel's ex-girlfriend, as a result of her being a fan of *Shaun of the Dead*.

Jim Broadbent similarly revealed his interest in *Shaun* and requested a role while meeting with Simon Pegg at a BAFTA awards ceremony.

Wright met with director Peter Jackson while he was filming *King Kong*, and Jackson suggested that he would be willing to do a cameo in the film. Edgar had Jackson wear a fake beard and pads to portray Father Christmas who stabs Angel in the opening montage.

In the same opening montage, Garth Jennings can be seen as a drug dealer, with the audio commentary stating Garth and Edgar Wright had an agreement to have cameo appearances in each other's films.

Production
Script
Wright decided that he wanted to write and direct a cop film because "there isn't really any tradition of cop films in the UK... We felt that every other country in the world had its own tradition of great cop action films and we had none." Wright and Simon Pegg spent eighteen months writing the script. The first draft took eight months to develop, and after watching 138 cop-related films for

dialogue and plot ideas and conducting over fifty interviews with police officers for research, the script was completed after another nine months. The title was based on the various two-word titles of action films in the 1980s and 90s. In one interview Wright declared that he "wanted to make a title that really had very little meaning...like *Lethal Weapon* and *Point Break* and *Executive Decision*." In the same interview, Pegg joked that when the many action films' titles were chosen that "...all those titles seem to be generated from two hats filled with adjectives and nouns and you just, 'Okay, that'll do.'" Pegg and Wright have referred to *Hot Fuzz* as being the second film in "The Three Flavours Cornetto Trilogy" with *Shaun of the Dead* as the first and future project *The World's End* as the third.

Preparation and filming

Simon Pegg filming in Wells

To prepare for their roles in the film, Simon Pegg and Nick Frost had to follow certain requirements. Pegg's contract stated that he had to adopt a strict diet and use three personal trainers to prepare him for the physically demanding scenes in the film. Frost was asked by Wright and Pegg to watch around twenty action films to warm him up for his role as a police officer, but he decided to only watch *Bad Boys II*.

During the latter half of 2005, Working Title approached several towns in South West England looking for an appropriate filming location. Simon Pegg commented "We're both from the West Country so it just seemed like it was the perfect and logical thing to drag those kind of ideas and those genres and those clichés back to our beginnings to where we grew up, so you could see high-octane balls-to-the-wall action in Frome". Stow-on-the-Wold was considered amongst others, but after being turned away, the company settled upon Wells in Somerset, Wright's hometown. Wright has commented "and Wells is very picturesque...I love it but I also want to trash it". The Wells Cathedral was digitally painted out of every shot of the village, as Wright wanted the Church of St. Cuthbert to be the centre building for the fictional town of Sandford (Sandford is also the fictional town name used during National Police Training when any role-playing exercises are taking place); however, the Bishop's Palace is identifiable in some shots. Filming also took place at the Hendon Police College, including the driving school skid pan and athletic track. While shooting scenes in their uniforms, Simon Pegg and Nick Frost were often mistaken for genuine police officers and asked for directions by passers-by. Filming commenced on 19 March 2006 and lasted for eleven weeks. After editing, Wright ended up cutting half an hour of footage from the film.

Homage

Wright has said that *Hot Fuzz* takes elements from his final amateur film, *Dead Right*, which he described as both "*Lethal Weapon* set in Somerset" and "a *Dirty Harry* film in Somerset". He uses some of the same locations in both films including the Somerfield supermarket, where he used to work as a shelf-stacker. In the scene in the Somerfield store, when Angel is confronting a chav for shoplifting, a DVD copy of *Shaun of the Dead* can be seen for a few frames. The title is *Zombies' Party*, the Spanish and Portuguese title for the film. Further homages to *Shaun of the Dead* are also present in the film. In one scene, Nicholas wants to chase a suspect down by jumping over garden fences, however Danny is reluctant. Nicholas responds "What's the matter Butterman? Never taken a shortcut before?" while smiling arrogantly before jumping over them. When Danny attempts it, he trips and falls through the fence. It is almost identical to a scene in *Shaun of the Dead*, including the fall-through-fence gag (in *Shaun of the Dead* however, it happens to Simon Pegg's character rather than Nick Frost's, and he falls over the fence rather than through it). Also, Nick Frost's character (Danny in *Hot Fuzz*, Ed in *Shaun of the Dead*) has an obsession with Cornettos.

Various scenes in *Hot Fuzz* feature a variety of action film DVDs such as *Supercop*, and scenes from *Point Break* and *Bad Boys II*. Wright revealed that he had to get permission from every actor in each video clip, including stunt men, to use the clips and for the use of the DVD covers had to pay for the rights from the respective studios. The film parodies clichés used in other action movies. On the topic of perceived gun fetishes in these movies, Pegg has said "Men can't do that thing, which is the greatest achievement of humankind, which is to make another human, so we make metal versions of our own penises and fire more bits of metal out of the end into people's heads...It's our turn to grab the gun by the hilt and fire it into your face." Despite this, Pegg maintains that the film is not a spoof in that, "They lack the sneer that a lot of parodies have that look down on their source material. Because we're looking up to it." The film also includes various references to *The Wicker Man*, in which Edward Woodward, here playing a major villain, had played a policeman tough on law and order.

Effects

Ten artists were used to develop the visual effects for the film. To illustrate the destruction of the mansion as a result of the gas explosion, gas mortars were placed in front of the building to create large-scale fireballs. The wave of fire engulfs the camera, and to achieve that effect, gas mortars were used again but were fired upwards into a black ceiling piece that sloped up towards the camera. When the sequence was shot at a high speed the flames appeared to surge across the ground. For one of the final scenes of the film, the Sandford police station is destroyed by an explosion. Part of the explosion was created by using a set model that showed its windows being blown out, while the building remained intact. The actual destruction of the building was depicted by exploding a miniature model of the station.

Similar to the work in *Shaun of the Dead*, blood and gore was prevalent throughout the film. Visual effects supervisor Richard Briscoe revealed the rationale for using the large amounts of blood: "In many ways, the more extreme you make it, the more people know it is stylised and enjoy the humour inherent in how ridiculous it is. It's rather like the (eventually) limbless Black Knight in *Monty Python's Holy Grail*." The most time-consuming gore sequence involved a character's head being crushed by a section of a church. A dummy was used against a green screen and the head was detonated at the point when the object was about to impact the body. Throughout the film, over seventy gunfight shots were digitally augmented; Briscoe's rationale for adding the additional effects was that "The town square shootout, for example, is full of extra little hits scattered throughout, so that it feels like our hero characters really do have it all going off, all around them. It was a great demonstration of [how] seemingly very trivial enhancements can make a difference when combined across a sequence."

Promotion

The first two teaser trailers were released on 16 October 2006. Wright, Pegg, and Frost maintained several video blogs which were released at various times throughout the production of the film. Wright and Frost held a panel at the 2006 Comic-Con convention in San Diego, California to promote *Hot Fuzz*, which included preliminary footage and a question and answer session. The two returned to the convention again in 2007 to promote the US DVD release. Advance screenings of the film took place on 14 February 2007 in the UK and the world premiere was on 16 February 2007. The premiere included escorts from motorcycle police officers and the use of blue carpet instead of the traditional red carpet.

Release

Critical reception

The film met with critical acclaim, and was rated as highly as *Shaun of the Dead*. It has a 91% "Certified Fresh" rating on Rotten Tomatoes and has a Metacritic score of 81/100. Olly Richards of *Empire* said of Simon Pegg and Nick Frost: "After almost a decade together they're clearly so comfortable in each other's presence that they feel no need to fight for the punchline, making them terrific company for two hours". Johnny Vaughan of *The Sun* already called it the "most arresting Britcom of 2007". Phillip French of *The Observer*, who did not care for *Shaun of the Dead*, warmed to the comedy team in this film. The film also received positive reviews stateside. Derek Elley of *Variety* praised Broadbent and Dalton, "[who] are especially good as Angel's hail-fellow-well-met superior and oily No. 1 suspect". As a homage to the genre, the film was well received by screenwriter Shane Black. On Spill.com, it got their 2nd-highest rating of 'Full Price!!'.

The Daily Mirror only gave *Hot Fuzz* 2/5, stating that "many of the jokes miss their target" as the film becomes more action-based. *Daily Mail* also shared *The Mirror*'s view, saying that "It's the lack of any serious intent that means too much of it is desperately unamusing, and unamusingly desperate". Anthony Quinn of *The Independent* said "The same impish spirit [as *Spaced*] is uncorked here, but it has been fatally indulged".

Box office

The film generated £7.1 million in its first weekend of release in the UK on 14 February 2007. In the 20 April US opening weekend, the film grossed $5.8 million from only 825 theatres, making it the highest per-theatre average of any film in the top ten that week. Its opening weekend take beat the $3.3 million opening weekend gross of Pegg and Wright's previous film, *Shaun of the Dead*. In its second weekend of release, Rogue Pictures expanded the film's theater count from 825 to 1,272 and it grossed $4.9 million, representing a 17% dip in the gross. Altogether, *Hot Fuzz* grossed $80,573,774 worldwide. In nine weeks, the film earned nearly twice what *Shaun of the Dead* made in the US, and more than three times its gross in other countries.

Home media

The DVD was released on 11 June 2007 in the UK. Over one million DVDs were sold in the UK in the first four weeks of its release. The two-disc set contains the feature film with commentaries, outtakes, storyboards, deleted scenes, a making-of documentary, video blogs, featurettes, galleries, and some hidden easter eggs. The DVD also features Wright's last amateur film, *Dead Right*, which he described as "*Hot Fuzz* without the budget". Due to the above release date, the film arrived on region 2 DVD earlier than the theatrical release date in Germany on 14 June 2007. In the commentary with director Edgar Wright and fellow filmmaker Quentin Tarantino they discuss nearly 200 films.

The US DVD and HD DVD release was on 31 July 2007. It opened at #2 at the American DVD sales chart, selling 853,000 units for over $14m in revenue. As per the latest figures, 1,923,000 units have been sold, acquiring revenue of $33.3m. The HD DVD edition has more special features than the standard DVD release. A three-disc collector's edition was released on 27 November 2007 and a Blu-ray edition on 22 September 2009.

Soundtrack

The soundtrack album, *Hot Fuzz: Music from the Motion Picture*, was released on 19 February 2007 in the United Kingdom, and on 17 April 2007 in the United States and Canada. The UK release contains 22 tracks, and the North American release has 14. The film's score is by British composer David Arnold, who has scored the James Bond film series since 1997. The soundtrack album's "Hot Fuzz Suite" is a compilation of excerpts from Arnold's score. According to the DVD commentary, the scenes where Nicholas Angel is at a convenience store, while leaving Sandford, and his return to the Police Station while arming for the final shootout (found in the track "Avenging Angel"), were scored by Robert Rodríguez, who didn't see the rest of the film while writing the music.

Other music from the film is a mix of 1960s and 1970s British rock (The Kinks, T.Rex, The Move, The Sweet, The Troggs, Arthur Brown, Cloud 69, Cozy Powell), New Wave (Adam Ant, XTC) and Glaswegian indie band (The Fratellis). The soundtrack album features dialogue extracts by Simon Pegg, Nick Frost, and other cast members, mostly embedded in the music tracks. The song selection also includes some police-themed titles, including Supergrass' "Caught by the Fuzz" as well as "Here Come the Fuzz", which was specially composed for the film by Jon Spencer's Blues Explosion.

Source http://en.wikipedia.org/wiki/Hot_Fuzz

Scott Pilgrim vs. the World

Scott Pilgrim vs. the World

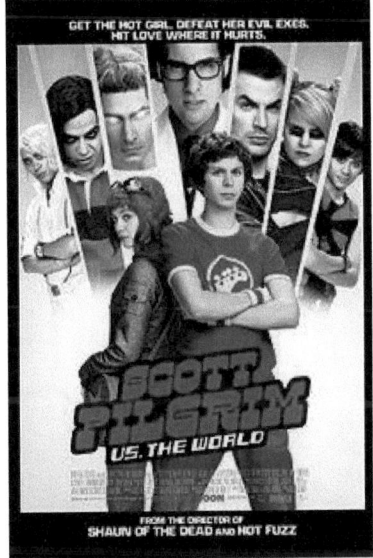

Official international poster

Directed by	Edgar Wright
Produced by	Edgar Wright Marc Platt Eric Gitter Nira Park
Screenplay by	Edgar Wright Michael Bacall
Based on	*Scott Pilgrim* by Bryan Lee O'Malley
Narrated by	Bill Hader
Starring	Michael Cera Mary Elizabeth Winstead Kieran Culkin Chris Evans Anna Kendrick Alison Pill Brandon Routh Jason Schwartzman
Music by	Nigel Godrich
Cinematography	Bill Pope
Editing by	Jonathan Amos Paul Machliss
Studio	Big Talk Films
Distributed by	Universal Pictures
Release date(s)	July 27, 2010 (Fan Festival) August 13, 2010 (United States)
Running time	112 minutes
Country	United States
Language	English
Budget	$85–90 million $60 million after tax rebates
Box office	$47,664,559

Scott Pilgrim vs. the World is a 2010 American comedy film directed by Edgar Wright, based on the graphic novel series *Scott Pilgrim* by Bryan Lee O'Malley. The film is about Scott Pilgrim, a young Canadian musician, meeting the girl of his dreams, Ramona Flowers, an American delivery girl. In order to win Ramona, Scott learns that he must defeat Ramona's "seven evil exes", who are coming to kill him.

Scott Pilgrim vs. the World was planned as a film after the first volume of the comic was released. Wright became attached to the project and filming began in March 2009 in Toronto. *Scott Pilgrim vs. the World* premiered after a panel discussion at the San Diego Comic-Con International on July 22, 2010. It received a wide release in North America on August 13, 2010, in 2,818 theaters. The film finished fifth on its first weekend of release with a total of $10.5 million. The film received generally positive reviews by critics and fans of the graphic novel, but it failed to recoup its production budget during its release in theaters, grossing $31.5 million in North America and $16 million overseas. However, the film has fared better on home video, becoming the top-selling Blu-ray Disc on Amazon.com during the first day it was available and has since gained a cult following.

Plot

In Toronto, Scott Pilgrim, the bass guitarist for the band "Sex Bob-omb", begins dating high schooler Knives Chau, much to the disapproval of his friends. Scott meets an American girl, Ramona Flowers, who has been appearing in his dreams, and becomes obsessed with her, losing interest in Knives. While playing in a battle of the bands sponsored by one "G-Man Graves" for a record deal, Scott is attacked by Matthew Patel, who introduces himself as the first of Ramona's "evil exes". Scott defeats Patel and learns from Ramona that, in order for them to date, he must defeat all seven of her evil exes.

Scott breaks up with Knives, who blames Ramona for taking Scott from her and begins trying to win him back. Scott battles Ramona's second evil ex, popular actor and skateboarder Lucas Lee, who he defeats by tricking him into performing a dangerous skateboard grind that causes him to combust. Scott later encounters the third evil ex, Todd Ingram, who is dating Scott's ex-girlfriend, Natalie "Envy" Adams. Todd initially overpowers Scott using his psychic vegan abilities, but is stripped of his powers by the Vegan Police after Scott tricks him into drinking coffee with half and half cream, allowing Scott to defeat him.

Scott begins to grow upset with Ramona over her dating history by the defeat of the fourth ex, Roxy Richter. During the second round of the battle of the bands, Sex Bob-omb faces off against the fifth and sixth evil exes, twin Katayanagi brothers Kyle and Ken, earning Scott an extra life upon their defeat. During the battle, Scott sees Ramona together with her seventh evil ex, Gideon Graves, who turns out to be Sex Bob-omb's sponsor, G-Man. The members of Sex Bob-omb accept Gideon's record deal, except for Scott, who leaves the band. Shortly after, Ramona breaks up with Scott.

Upon returning home, Scott receives a phone call invitation from Gideon to his newly opened Chaos Theater where Sex Bob-omb is playing, claiming there to be "no hard feelings". Scott arrives and challenges Gideon to a fight, professing his love for Ramona and gaining a sword called the "Power of Love", which Gideon easily destroys. Knives then crashes the scene to fight Ramona over Scott. Scott goes to break up the girls' fight, only to accidentally reveal that he cheated on them with each other before he is killed by Gideon.

Ramona visits Scott in Limbo and apologizes for getting him involved in her affairs, revealing that Gideon had planted a mind control device in the back of her head. Scott realizes he still has an extra life and uses it to return to life at the moment in time when Gideon first called him. Scott reenters the Chaos Theater where he makes peace with his friends and challenges Gideon again, stating he is fighting for himself and gaining the much stronger "Power of Self-Respect" sword with which he strikes down Gideon. He then apologizes to Ramona and Knives for cheating on them, but Gideon interferes and knocks down Ramona, leading Scott and Knives to team up and defeat him. Free from Gideon's control, Ramona prepares to leave, but Knives accepts that her relationship with Scott is over and encourages him to follow Ramona. He does, and the two start their relationship anew.

Cast

Main characters

Michael Cera as Scott Pilgrim, a 23-year-old Canadian, who falls in love with Ramona Flowers. He is the bass guitarist of the band Sex Bob-omb.

Mary Elizabeth Winstead as Ramona Flowers, a mysterious American delivery girl with a dating history that drives the plot of the film.

Kieran Culkin as Wallace Wells, Scott's 25-year-old gay roommate and close friend.

Ellen Wong as Knives Chau, a 17-year-old high school girl whom Scott dates before meeting Ramona.

Alison Pill as Kim Pine, the 23-year-old drummer of Sex Bob-omb and one of Scott's ex-girlfriends.

Mark Webber as Stephen Stills, the 22-year-old lead singer and "talent" of the Sex Bob-omb.

Johnny Simmons as "Young" Neil Nordegraf, a 20-year-old fan of Sex Bob-omb and Scott's replacement after he leaves the band.

Anna Kendrick as Stacey Pilgrim, Scott's 18-year-old sister; she refers to Scott as her "little brother", this may be because she is notably wiser and more intelligent than her older brother.

Brie Larson as Natalie "Envy" Adams, one of Scott's ex-girlfriends who went on to become the singer of the successful band The Clash at Demonhead.

Aubrey Plaza as Julie Powers, Stephen's obnoxious ex-girlfriend.

The League of Evil Exes, in numerical order

Satya Bhabha as Matthew Patel, who has mystical powers, such as fireballs and levitation

Chris Evans as Lucas Lee, a "pretty good" skateboarder turned "pretty good" action movie star.

Brandon Routh as Todd Ingram, the bassist for The Clash at Demonhead who possesses telekinetic powers as a result of his veganism; he is the boyfriend of Scott's ex-girlfriend Envy Adams.

Mae Whitman as Roxanne "Roxy" Richter, a self-conscious lesbian half-ninja.

Shota and Keita Saito as Kyle Katayanagi and Ken Katayanagi, twins and popular Japanese musicians.

Jason Schwartzman as Gideon Gordon Graves, manager of the Chaos Theatre, Sex Bob-omb's sponsor and the mastermind behind the League of Evil Exes.

Other characters

Kjartan Hewitt as Jimmy, Stacey's boyfriend; Wallace stole him and the two kiss as Ramona leaves the first round of the Battle of the Bands at the "Rockit"; from Stacey's reaction, it is implied that Wallace has done this before

Ben Lewis as Other Scott, another one of Wallace's boyfriends

Nelson Franklin as Michael Comeau, one of Scott's friends who "knows everybody"

Christine Watson as Matthew Patel's Demon Hipster Chicks

Chantelle Chung as Tamara Chen, Knives' best friend

Don McKellar as Director, the director of the Lucas Lee film

Emily Kassie as Winifred Hailey, a 16-year-old actress who was due to star in a film with Lucas Lee before he was defeated by Scott; she briefly appears on the film set at the Casa Loma

John Patrick Amedori as the Chaos Theatre's bouncer

Tennessee Thomas as Lynette Guycott, drummer for The Clash at Demonhead.

Erik Knudsen as Luke "Crash" Wilson, singer and guitarist of the band Crash and the Boys who competes in the battle of the bands.

Maurie W. Kaufmann as Joel, a member of Crash and the Boys

Abigail Chu as Trisha "Trasha" Ha, the 8-year-old drummer of Crash and the Boys

Kristina Pesic and Ingrid Haas as Sandra and Monique, two popular girls at Julie's party

Thomas Jane and Clifton Collins, Jr. appear uncredited as the Vegan Policemen. The author, Bryan Lee O'Malley, and his wife, Hope Larson, also appear uncredited as Lee's Palace bar patrons.

Reuben Langdon (known for being the voices of Ken in *Street Fighter IV*, and Dante in the *Devil May Cry* series) has a cameo as one of Lucas Lee's stunt doubles.

Production

Development

After artist Bryan Lee O'Malley completed the first volume of *Scott Pilgrim*, his publisher Oni Press contacted producer Marc Platt with the proposition for a film version. Universal Studios contracted Edgar Wright who had just finished his last film, *Shaun of the Dead*, to adapt the *Scott Pilgrim* comics. O'Malley originally had mixed feelings about a film adaptation, stating that he "expected them to turn it into a full-on action comedy with some actor that I hated" [but ultimately] "didn't even care. I was a starving artist, and I was like, 'Please, just give me some money.'"

In May 2005, the studio signed Michael Bacall to write the screenplay adaptation. Bacall said that he wanted to write the *Scott Pilgrim* film because he "felt strongly" about the story and "empathized" with *Scott Pilgrim*'s characters. By January 2009, filmmakers rounded out its cast for the film, now titled *Scott Pilgrim vs. the World*. Edgar Wright noted that O'Malley was "very involved" with the script of the film from the start, and even contributed lines to and "polished" certain scenes in the film. Likewise, due to the long development process, several lines from the various scripts written by Wright and Bacall ended up in books four and five as well.

O'Malley confirmed that no material from *Scott Pilgrim's Finest Hour*, the sixth Scott Pilgrim volume, would appear in the film, as production had already begun. While he had given ideas and suggestions for the final act of the film, he admitted to that some of those plans might change throughout the writing process and ultimately stated that "Their ending is their ending". O'Malley gave Wright and Bacall his notes for the sixth book while filming took place.

Casting of the principal characters began in June 2008. Principal photography began in March 2009 in Toronto and wrapped as scheduled in August. In the film's original ending, written before the release of the final *Scott Pilgrim* book, Scott ultimately gets back together with Knives. After the final book in the series was released, in which Scott and Ramona get back together, and negative audience reaction to the ending during testing, a new ending was filmed to match the books, with Scott and Ramona getting back together.

The film was given a production budget of $85–90 million, an amount offset by tax rebates that resulted in a final cost around $60 million. Universal fronted $60 million of the pre-rebate budget.

Casting

Director Wright felt confident with his casting in the film. Wright stated that "Like with *Hot Fuzz* how we had great people in every single tiny part, it's the same with this. What's great with this is that there's people you know, like with Michael [Cera] and Jason [Schwartzman], and then we have people who are up and coming, like Anna Kendrick, Aubrey Plaza and Brie Larson, and then there's complete unknowns as well". There was no studio interference with casting more unknowns, as Wright stated that "Universal never really gave me any problems about casting bigger people, because in a way Michael [Cera] has starred in two $100 million-plus movies, and also a lot of the other people, though they're not the biggest names, people certainly know who they are." Wright planned on casting Cera while writing *Hot Fuzz* after watching episodes of *Arrested Development*. Wright said he needed an actor that "audiences will still follow even when the character is being a bit of an ass." Edgar Wright ran all his casting decisions by O'Malley during the casting session. Mary Elizabeth Winstead was Wright's choice for Ramona Flowers two years before filming had started, because "she has a very sunny disposition as a person, so it was interesting to get her to play a version of herself that was broken inside. She's great in the film because she causes a lot of chaos but remains supernaturally grounded." Ellen Wong, a Toronto actress known mostly from a role in *This Is Wonderland*, auditioned for the part of Knives Chau three times. On her second audition, Wright learned that Wong has a green belt in tae kwon do, and says he found himself intrigued by this "sweet-faced young lady being a secret badass".

Music

Radiohead producer Nigel Godrich, Beck, Metric, Broken Social Scene, Cornelius, Dan the Automator, Kid Koala, and David Campbell all contributed to the film's soundtrack. Beck wrote and composed the music played by Sex Bob-omb in the film, and two unreleased songs can also be heard in the teaser trailer. Cast members Mark Webber, Alison Pill and Johnny Simmons all had to learn to play their respective instruments, and spent time rehearsing as a band with Michael Cera (who already played bass) and Beck before filming began. The actors also perform on the movie soundtrack. Brendan Canning and Kevin Drew of Broken Social Scene wrote all the songs for Crash and the Boys. The tracks were sung by actor Erik Knudsen, who plays Crash in the film. Drew stated that the reason behind this was that "[he] knew that [Knudsen] didn't need to be a singer to pull [it] off" because the songs were "so quick and punk and fast" and "it needed to be the character's voice." Metric is the inspiration for the film's fictional band, the Clash at Demonhead, and contributed the song "Black Sheep" to the film. The clothing of Metric's lead singer, Emily Haines, is also the basis for the clothing of the lead singer of Clash at Demonhead. Brie Larson provides the vocals for "Black Sheep" in the film, while the soundtrack features a version of the song with Haines as lead singer. Chris Murphy of the band Sloan was the guitar coach for the actors in the film. Music from *The Legend of Zelda* video game series is used in a dream sequence in the film. To get permission to use the music, Edgar Wright sent a clip of the film and wrote a letter to Nintendo that described the music as "like nursery rhymes to a generation."

Title sequence
The opening title sequence was designed by Richard Kenworthy of Shynola, and was inspired by the drawn-on-film animation work of Len Lye, Oskar Fischinger, Stan Brakhage, and Norman McLaren.

Release

Michael Cera dressed as Captain America at the *Scott Pilgrim* panel at the San Diego Comic-Con.

A *Scott Pilgrim vs. the World* panel featured at the San Diego Comic-Con International held on July 22, 2010. After the panel Edgar Wright invited selected members of the audience for a screening of the film which was followed by a performance by Metric. *Scott Pilgrim vs. the World* was also shown at the Fantasia Festival in Montreal, Quebec, Canada on July 27, 2010 and was also featured at the Movie-Con III in London, England on August 15, 2010.

The film premiered in Japan during the Yubari International Fantastic Film Festival on February 26, 2011 as an official selection. It was released to the rest of the country on April 29, 2011.

Marketing
On March 25, 2010, the first teaser trailer for the film was released.

A second trailer featuring music by The Ting Tings, LCD Soundsystem, Be Your Own Pet, Cornelius, Blood Red Shoes, and The Prodigy was released May 31, 2010.

At the 2010 MTV Movie Awards, the first clip was released featuring Scott Pilgrim facing Lucas Lee in battle. The actors playing Lucas Lee's stunt doubles are the actual stunt doubles for Chris Evans. Alison Pill who plays Kim Pine in the film stated that her character's past relationship with Scott will be explored in other media stating that "There will be a little something-something that will air on Adult Swim". The animated short, *Scott Pilgrim vs. the Animation*, produced by Titmouse Inc., adapts the opening prologue of the second *Scott Pilgrim* book and was aired on Adult Swim on August 12, 2010, later being released on their website. Michael Cera stated that he felt the film was "a tricky one to sell. I don't know how you convey that movie in a marketing campaign. I can see it being something that people are slow to discover. In honesty, I was slow to find *Shaun of the Dead*".

Video game
A video game was produced based on the series. It was released for PlayStation Network on August 10, 2010 and on Xbox Live Arcade on August 25, being met with mostly positive reviews. The game is published by Ubisoft and developed by Ubisoft Montreal and Ubisoft Chengdu, featuring animation by Paul Robertson and original music by Anamanaguchi.

Home media
Scott Pilgrim vs. the World was released on DVD and Blu-ray Disc in North America on November 9, 2010 and in the United Kingdom on December 27, 2010.

The DVD features include four audio commentaries: (director Wright, co-writer Bacall, and author O'Malley; Wright and director of photography Pope; Cera, Schwartzman, Winstead, Wong, and Routh; and Kendrick, Plaza, Culkin, and Webber), 21 deleted, extended, and alternate scenes including the original ending (where Scott ends up with Knives) with commentary, bloopers, photo galleries, and a trivia track.

The Blu-ray Disc release includes all DVD features, plus alternate footage, six featurettes, production blogs, *Scott Pilgrim vs. the Animation*, trailers and TV spots, storyboard picture-in-picture, a DVD copy, and a digital copy. The "Ultimate Japan Version" Blu-ray Disc includes a commentary track that features Wright and Shinya Arino. It also includes footage of Wright and Michael Cera's publicity tour through Japan and a roundtable discussion with Japanese film critic Tomohiro Machiyama. It was released on September 2, 2011.

In its first week of release, the DVD sold 190,217 copies, earning $3,422,004 in revenue. It reached the top of the UK Blu-ray Disc charts in its first week of release.

Reception

Box office
The film was widely released in North America on August 13, 2010, opening in 2,818 theaters. The film finished fifth on its first weekend of release with a total of $10.5 million, and by its second weekend of release had dropped to the bottom of the top ten. *The Wall Street Journal* described this as "disappointing" while Ben Fritz of the *Los Angeles Times* noted that the film appeared to be a "major financial disappointment". Universal acknowledged their disappointment at the opening weekend, saying they had "been aware of the challenges of broadening this film to a mainstream audience"; regardless, the studio's spokesman said Universal was "proud of this film and our relationship with the visionary and creative filmmaker Edgar Wright.... Edgar has created a truly unique film that is both envelope pushing and genre bending and when examined down the road will be identified as an important piece of filmmaking."

In the UK, the film opened in 408 cinemas, finishing second on its opening weekend with £1.6 million, dropping to fifth place by the next weekend.

Critical response
Critical response to the film has been positive. Review aggregation website Rotten Tomatoes gives the film a score

of 81% based on 217 reviews, with an average score of 7.5 out of 10. Rotten Tomatoes' consensus is that "its script may not be as dazzling as its eye-popping visuals, but *Scott Pilgrim vs. the World* is fast, funny, and inventive".

Metacritic has assigned an average score of 69, based on 38 reviews, which indicates generally favorable reviews. David Edelstein of *New York* magazine wrote that "The film is repetitive, top-heavy: Wright blows his wad too early. But a different lead might have kept you laughing and engaged. Cera doesn't come alive in the fight scenes the way Stephen Chow does in the best (and most Tashlin-like) of all the surreal martial-arts comedies, *Kung Fu Hustle*."

At a test screening, director Kevin Smith was impressed by the film saying "That movie is great. It's spellbinding and nobody is going to understand what the fuck just hit them. I would be hard pressed to say, 'he's bringing a comic book to life!' but he is bringing a comic book to life." Smith also said that fellow directors Quentin Tarantino and Jason Reitman were "really into it". Singer for the band Sister and writer for *Now*, Carla Gillis, also commented on the film. Gillis was the singer of the now-disbanded Canadian group Plumtree, and their single "Scott Pilgrim" that inspired O'Malley to create the character and the series. In an interview describing the film and the song that inspired it, Gillis felt the film carried the same positive yet bittersweet tone of the song.

After premiere screenings at the San Diego Comic-Con International, the film received positive reviews. *Variety* gave the film a mixed review, referring to the film as "An example of attention-deficit filmmaking at both its finest and its most frustrating" and that "anyone over 25 is likely to find director Edgar Wright's adaptation of the cult graphic novel exhausting, like playing chaperone at a party full of oversexed college kids."

The Hollywood Reporter wrote a negative review, stating that "What's disappointing is that this is all so juvenile. Nothing makes any real sense..[Michael] Cera doesn't give a performance that anchors the nonsense." and "Universal should have a youth hit in the domestic market when the film opens next month. A wider audience among older or international viewers seems unlikely."

IGN gave the film a positive rating of 8/10 calling the film "funny and offbeat" as well as noting that the film is "best suited for the wired generation and those of us who grew up on Nintendo and MTV. Its kinetic nature and quirky sensibilities might be a turnoff for some."

Nick Schager of *Slant Magazine* gave the film a positive review of three and a half stars out of four, calling Edgar Wright an "inspired mash-up artist, and *Scott Pilgrim vs. the World* may be his finest hybridization to date". A. O. Scott made the film his "critics pick", stating "There are some movies about youth that just make you feel old, even if you aren't...*Scott Pilgrim vs. the World* has the opposite effect. Its speedy, funny, happy-sad spirit is so infectious that the movie makes you feel at home in its world even if the landscape is, at first glance, unfamiliar."

After its premiere in Japan, several notable video game, film, and anime industry personalities have praised *Scott Pilgrim vs. the World*, among them Hironobu Sakaguchi, Goichi Suda, Miki Mizuno, Tomohiko Itō, Rintaro Watanabe and Takao Nakano.

Accolades

The film received four nominations at the 2010 Satellite Awards held on December 19, 2010 at the Intercontinental Hotel in Century City. It won in two categories; Best film – Comedy or Musical and Best Actor – Musical or Comedy for Michael Cera. The film also made the final short list for a nomination for Best Visual Effects at the 83rd Academy Awards, but did not receive a nomination.

Awards

Award	Category	Name
83rd Academy Awards	Best Visual Effects	
Artios Awards	Outstanding Achievement in Casting – Big Budget Feature – Comedy	Robin D. Cook and Jennifer Euston
Austin Film Critics Association Awards	Best film	
Central Ohio Film Critics Association	Best Picture	
	Best Overlooked Film	
Detroit Film Critics Society Awards	Best Director	Edgar Wright
	Best Ensemble	Overall cast-ing
Empire Awards	Best Film	
	Best Sci-Fi/Fantasy	
	Best Director	Edgar Wright
GLAAD Media Awards	Outstanding Film – Wide Release	
Hugo Awards	Best Dramatic Presentation – Long Form	Michael Bacall and Edgar Wright
Sierra Awards	Best Art Direction	
	Best Costume Design	Laura Jean Shannon
	Best Song	Beck for "We Are Sex Bob-Omb"
	Best Visual Effects	
Online Film Critics Society Awards	Best Editing	Jonathan Amos and Paul Machliss
	Best Adapted Screenplay	Michael Bacall and Edgar Wright
SFX Awards	Best Film Director	Edgar Wright
San Diego Film Critics Society Awards	Best Editing	Jonathan Amos and Paul Machliss
	Best Adapt-	Michael Ba

	ed Screenplay	call and Edgar Wright		tor Best Scream-Play	Wright		Fight Scene of the Year	Final Battle Scott Pilgrim and Knives vs. Gideon Graves
Satellite Awards	Best Film – Musical or Comedy			Best Villain	Satya Bhabha, Chris Evans, Brandon Routh, Mae Whitman, Shota Saito, Keita Saito and Jason Schwartzman as The League of Evil Exes		Best Comic Book Movie	
	Best Actor – Motion Picture Musical or Comedy	Michael Cera				Teen Choice Awards	Choice Movie: Action Actor	Michael Cera
	Best Art Direction and Production Design	Nigel Churcher and Marcus Rowland					Choice Movie: Action Actress	Mary Elizabeth Winstead
	Best Adapted Screenplay	Michael Bacall and Edgar Wright					Choice Movie: Action	
						Utah Film Critics Association Awards	Best Director	Edgar Wright
Saturn Awards	Best Fantasy Film			Best Supporting Actress	Ellen Wong		Best Screenplay	Michael Bacall and Edgar Wright
Scream Awards	The Ultimate Scream			Best Supporting Actor	Kieran Culkin			
	Best Director	Edgar				Source	http://en.wikipedia.org/wiki/Scott_Pilgrim_vs._the_World	

Shaun of the Dead

Shaun of the Dead

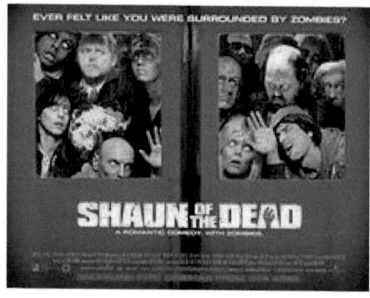

UK release poster

Directed by	Edgar Wright
Produced by	Nira Park
Written by	Edgar Wright Simon Pegg
Starring	Simon Pegg Kate Ashfield Lucy Davis Nick Frost Dylan Moran Bill Nighy Penelope Wilton
Music by	Pete Woodhead Daniel Mudford
Cinematography	David M. Dunlap
Editing by	Chris Dickens
Studio	StudioCanal Working Title Film Big Talk Productions Film4 Productions
Distributed by	Universal Pictures (Rogue Pictures (US
Release date(s)	9 April 2004 (United Kingdom) 24 April 2004 (United States)
Running time	99 minutes
Country	United Kingdom France
Language	English
Budget	£4,000,000
Box office	$30,039,392

Shaun of the Dead is a 2004 British zombie comedy directed and co-written by Edgar Wright, and co-written and starring Simon Pegg alongside Nick Frost. Pegg plays Shaun, a man attempting to get some kind of focus in his life as he deals with his girlfriend, his mother and stepfather. At the same time, he has to cope with an apocalyptic uprising of zombies.

The film is the first of what Pegg and Wright call The Three Flavours Cornetto Trilogy with *Hot Fuzz* (2007) as the second and *The World's End* (TBA) as the third.

The film was a critical and commercial success in the UK, and the US. It received a 91% approval rating on Rotten Tomatoes and a score of 76 out of 100 at Metacritic. *Shaun of the Dead* was a BAFTA nominee. Pegg and Wright considered a sequel that would replace zombies with another monster, but decided against it as they were pleased with the first film as a stand-alone product, and thought too many characters died to continue the story.

Plot

Shaun (Pegg) is a salesman whose life has no direction. His younger colleagues show him no respect, he has a rocky relationship with his stepfather, Phillip (Nighy), a tense relationship with his housemate, Pete (Serafinowicz), because of Ed (Frost), Shaun's crude best friend who lives on their couch and deals marijuana, and his girlfriend, Liz (Ashfield), is dissatisfied with their social life, as it consists primarily of spending every evening at the Winchester, Shaun and Ed's favourite pub. They never do anything alone together – Shaun always brings Ed, and Liz brings her flatmates, David (Moran) and Dianne (Davis).

After a miserable day at work, Shaun meets an old friend, Yvonne (Stevenson), who asks him what he and Liz are doing for their anniversary, which makes him realise he forgot to book a table at a restaurant, as he had promised to do. Faced with this, Liz breaks up with him. Shaun drowns his sorrows with Ed at the Winchester. The two return home late and spin electro records, only to have Pete confront them, who is suffering a headache after being mugged and bitten by "some crackheads". Pete berates Shaun and tells him to sort his life out. Shaun resolves to do so.

The next morning, an uprising of zombies has overwhelmed the town, but Shaun is too busy dealing with his problems and too hungover to notice. He and Ed become aware of what is happening after watching reports on TV, as zombies attack their house. After fighting back with weapons from the shed, they decide they need to go somewhere safe. Shaun and Ed decide that the safest place they know is the Winchester, and they plan to collect Shaun's mother, Barbara (Wilton), Phillip, Liz, and her flatmates. Shaun discovers that a naked Pete is still in the house and is now a zombie, and he and Ed escape in Pete's car. After collecting Barbara and Phillip, who is bitten in the process, they switch cars and drive in Phillip's Jaguar and head to Liz, Dianne and David's flat, and collect them. Before they make it to the Winchester, Phillip dies of his bite, after he manages to make peace with Shaun. Abandoning the car as Phillip turns into a zombie, they set off on foot, bumping into Yvonne and her own band of survivors. Discovering that the path is infested with zombies, they devise a plan to sneak by, but Ed and Shaun get into an argument and the zombies are alerted. David smashes the window while Shaun distracts the zombies. Everyone takes refuge inside the pub, and Shaun joins them after giving the zombies the slip.

After several hours, the zombies return. Ed gives away their position and the zombies converge on the pub. Shaun discovers that the Winchester rifle above the bar is functional and they use it to fend off the zombies. Barbara reveals a bite wound she picked up along the way and dies, becomes a zombie, and is reluctantly shot by a heartbroken Shaun. David is dismembered and disembowelled by the zombies, as a frantic Dianne unbolts the door to rescue him, exposing Shaun, Liz and Ed to the zombies. Ed prepares a Molotov cocktail to fend them off, but Pete arrives and bites him. He manages to get over the bar and Shaun uses the cocktail to set fire to the bar. They escape into the cellar. Trapped, they contemplate suicide, then discover a service hatch. Shaun and Liz escape through the hatch as a mortally wounded Ed stays behind with the rifle. Back on the street, as Shaun and Liz prepare to fight the zombies once more, the British Army arrives and they are rescued. Yvonne, who has also survived, shows up and tells Shaun and Liz to follow her. They approach the safety of the trucks, reconciled.

Six months after the outbreak, the uninfected have returned to daily life, while the remaining zombies, retaining their instincts, are used as cheap labour and entertainment. Liz and Shaun have moved in together in Shaun's house, and Shaun is keeping Ed, who is now a zombie, tethered in the shed and playing video games.

Cast

Simon Pegg as Shaun
Nick Frost as Ed
Kate Ashfield as Liz
Lucy Davis as Dianne
Dylan Moran as David
Penelope Wilton as Barbara
Bill Nighy as Phillip
Jessica Stevenson as Yvonne
Peter Serafinowicz as Pete
Rafe Spall as Noel
Martin Freeman as Declan
Reece Shearsmith as Mark
Tamsin Greig as Maggie
Julia Deakin as Yvonne's mum
Matt Lucas as Cousin Tom
Mark Donovan as Hulking Zombie

Production

The film is notable for Wright's kinetic directing style, and its references to other movies, television shows, and video games. In this way, it is similar to the British sitcom *Spaced*, which both Pegg and Wright worked on in similar roles.

The film was inspired by the *Spaced* episode "Art", written by Pegg (along with his writing partner and co-star Jessica Stevenson) and directed by Wright, in which the character of Tim (Pegg), under the influence of amphetamine and the PlayStation video game *Resident Evil 2*, hallucinates that he's fighting off a zombie invasion. Having discovered a mutual appreciation for Romero's *Dead* trilogy, they decided to write their own zombie movie. *Spaced* was to be a big influence on the making of *Shaun*, as it was directed by Wright in a similar style, and featured many of the same cast and crew in minor and major roles (as well as Pegg, Wright and Stevenson, Nick Frost — who played Mike in *Spaced* — has a starring role in *Shaun* as Ed, and Peter Serafinowicz and Julia Deakin, who played Duane Benzie and Marsha in *Spaced*, respectively — appeared in *Shaun* as Pete and Yvonne's mum, respectively).

The film's cast features a number of British comedians, comic actors and sitcom stars, most prominently from *Spaced*, *Black Books* and *The Office*. *Shaun* also co-stars Dylan Moran, who played Bernard Black in *Black Books*, and Lucy Davis, who played Dawn Tinsley in *The Office*. In addition to this, cameo appearances are made by Martin Freeman (Tim Canterbury in *The Office*), Tamsin Greig (Fran in *Black Books*, Caroline in *Green Wing*), Julia Deakin (Marsha in *Spaced*), Reece Shearsmith (Dexter in *Spaced* and a member of *The League of Gentlemen*) and Matt Lucas (writer/co-star of *Little Britain*). In addition, the voices of Mark Gatiss (*The League of Gentlemen*) and Julia Davis (*Nighty Night*) can be heard as radio news presenters, as can David Walliams (*Little Britain*) who provides the voice of an unseen TV reporter. Trisha Goddard also makes a cameo appearance, hosting a fictionalised episode of her real-life talk show *Trisha*. Many other comics and comic actors appear in cameos as zombies, including Rob Brydon, Paul Putner, Pamela Kempthorne (Morticia de'Ath in *The Vampires of Bloody Island*), Joe Cornish, Antonia Campbell-Hughes (from the Jack Dee sit com *Lead Balloon*), Mark Donovan (*Black Books*) and Michael Smiley (Tyres in *Spaced*). Coldplay members Chris Martin (who contributed to the soundtrack by guest singing the cover of Buzzcocks' "Everybody's Happy Nowadays" by Ash) and Jonny Buckland also cameo as zombies in the movie.

Locations

The production was filmed entirely in London, on location and at Ealing Studios, and involved production companies Working Title Films and StudioCanal. Many exterior shots were filmed in and around the North London areas of Crouch End, Muswell Hill and Finsbury Park. Zombie extras were mainly local residents or fans of *Spaced* who responded to a casting call organised through a fan website.

The scenes filmed in and around "The Winchester Pub" were shot at *The Duke Of Albany* in Monson Road New Cross, a three-storey Victorian pub popular with supporters of Millwall F.C. which was converted into luxury flats in 2007.

Reception

Box office

In the UK, *Shaun* took £1.6 million at 366 cinemas on its opening weekend and netted £6.4 million by mid-May. In its opening weekend in the US, *Shaun* earned $3.3 million, taking eighth place at the box office despite a limited release to only 607 theatres. The film has earned $30,039,392 worldwide in box office receipts since its release.

Critical response

Shaun of the Dead received positive critical reviews, with the film receiving a score of 91% at the comparative review website Rotten Tomatoes (with a Cream Of The Crop score of 94%) and a score of 76 out of 100 at Metacritic which indicates "generally favorable reviews". Nev Pierce, reviewing the film for the BBC, called it a "side-splitting, head-smashing, gloriously gory horror comedy" that will "amuse casual viewers and delight genre fans." Peter Bradshaw gave it four stars out of five, saying it "boasts a script crammed with real gags" and is "pacily directed [and] nicely acted."

Awards and recognition

In 2004, *Total Film* magazine named *Shaun of the Dead* the 49th greatest British film of all time. In 2005, it was rated as the third greatest comedy film of all time in a Channel 4 poll. Horror novelist Stephen King described the movie as "...a '10' on the fun meter and destined to be a cult classic." In 2007, *Stylus Magazine* named it the ninth-greatest zombie film ever made. In 2007, *Time* named it one of the 25 best horror films, calling the film "spooky, silly and smart-smart-smart" and complimenting its director: "Wright, who'd be a director to watch in any genre, plays world-class games with the camera and the viewer's expectations of what's supposed to happen in a scare film.". Bloody Disgusting ranked the film second in their list of the 'Top 20 Horror Films of the Decade', with the article saying "Shaun of the Dead isn't just the best horror-comedy of the decade – it's quite possibly the best horror-comedy ever made." In December 2009, Now Magazine deemed *Shaun of the Dead* the best film of the decade.

George A. Romero was so impressed with Pegg and Wright's work that he asked them to appear in cameo roles in the 2005 film *Land of the Dead*. Pegg and Wright insisted on being zombies rather than the slightly more noticeable roles that were originally offered.

Quentin Tarantino dubbed the film as one of his top twenty films made since 1992.

In March 2011, the film was voted by BBC Radio 1 and BBC Radio 1Xtra listeners as their second favourite film of all time. Frank Darabont's *The Shawshank Redemption* came in first place.

Home media

The film was released on DVD shortly after its theatrical run in the US, with a DVD release around December 2004 in the US. Features included several audio commentaries, EPK featurettes about the film's production, pre-production video diaries and concept videos, photo galleries, bloopers, and more. The film also saw release on the HD DVD format in July 2007, with a Blu-ray Disc release following in September 2009.

Merchandise

In 2006, the National Entertainment Collectibles Association announced that it would be producing action figures based on the film as part of its "Cult Classics" line that features fan favourite characters from various genre films. The releases so far are:

12" Shaun with sound

7" Shaun, which was released in Cult Classics series 4. The sculpt was based on the 12" figure.

"Winchester" two-pack, featuring 7" versions of Ed and a bloodied-up Shaun with the Winchester rifle.

Zombie Ed, which is a re-deco of the "Winchester" Ed, to be released in Cult Classics: Hall of Fame.

Upper Deck Entertainment released a card for the popular *World of Warcraft* Card Game in 2007, an ally named "Shawn of the Dead", with the power of bringing back allies from the enemy graveyard.

Cultural references

Prominent are many references to George A. Romero's earlier *Dead* films (*Night of the Living Dead*, *Dawn of the Dead* and *Day of the Dead*, with *Dawn* in particular being referenced). The title *Shaun of the Dead* is also both an obvious parody of and homage to the title *Dawn of the Dead*. Numerous lines, scenes and background details also directly refer to the Romero films, including the music playing over the Universal logo, a piece of synthesizer library music used during the hangar scene in *Dawn of the Dead*.

Soundtrack

Shaun of the Dead: Music from the Motion Picture

Soundtrack album by various artists

Released	12 April 2004
Genre	Rock
	Alternative rock
	Ska
	Hip-Hop
	Electro
Label	Universal International

Edgar Wright film soundtrack chronology

Shaun of the Dead (2004)	*Hot Fuzz* (2007)

Professional ratings

Review scores

Source	Rating
Allmusic	★★★★★

The film's score by Pete Woodhead and Daniel Mudford is a pastiche of Italian zombie film soundtracks by artists like Goblin and Fabio Frizzi. It also uses many musical cues from the original *Dawn of the Dead* that were originally culled by George A. Romero from the De Wolfe production music library.

On the soundtrack album, dialogue from the film is embedded within the music tracks.

"Figment" – S. Park
"The Blue Wrath" – I Monster
"Mister Mental" – The Eighties Matchbox B-Line Disaster
"Meltdown" – Ash
"Don't Stop Me Now" – Queen
"White Lines (Don't Don't Do It)" – Grandmaster Flash and the Furious Five and Melle Mel
"Hip Hop, Be Bop (Don't Stop)" – Man Parrish
"Zombie Creeping Flesh" – Pete Woodhead and Daniel Mudford
"Kernkraft 400" – Zombie Nation
"Fizzy Legs" – Pete Woodhead and Daniel Mudford
"Soft" – Lemon Jelly
"Death Bivouac" – Pete Woodhead and Daniel Mudford
"The Gonk (Kid Koala Remix)" – The Noveltones
"Envy the Dead" – Pete Woodhead and Daniel Mudford
"Ghost Town" – The Specials
"Blood in Three Flavours" – Pete Woodhead and Daniel Mudford
"Panic" – The Smiths
"Everybody's Happy Nowadays" – Ash featuring Chris Martin (Originally by Buzzcocks)
"You're My Best Friend" – Queen
"You've Got Red on You / Shaun of the Dead Suite" – Pete Woodhead and Daniel Mudford
"Normality" – Pete Woodhead and Daniel Mudford
"Fundead" – Pete Woodhead and Daniel Mudford
"Orpheus" – Ash

Comic strip

Pegg and Wright also scripted a one-off tie-in comic strip for the British comic magazine *2000AD* titled "There's Something About Mary".

Set the day before the zombie outbreak, the strip follows and expands on the character of Mary, who appears briefly in the introductory credits, and is the first zombie whom Shaun and Ed are aware of, and details how she became a zombie. It features expanded appearances from many of the minor or background characters who appear in the film. The strip was made available on the DVD release of *Shaun*, along with two other strips that wrapped up "Plot Holes" in the film, like how Diane escaped and survived the Winchester incident, and Ed's fate after taking refuge in the basement of the bar.

Source http://en.wikipedia.org/wiki/Shaun_of_the_Dead

The World's End

The World's End

The World's End

Teaser Poster

Directed by	Edgar Wright
Produced by	Nira Park Tim Bevan Eric Fellner
Written by	Edgar Wright Simon Pegg
Starring	Simon Pegg Nick Frost
Music by	Steven Price
Studio	StudioCanal Working Title Films Big Talk Productions
Distributed by	Universal Pictures
Release date(s)	14 August 2013 (UK) 25 October 2013 (US)
Country	United Kingdom France
Language	English

The World's End is a forthcoming British comedy film directed by Edgar Wright, co-written by Wright and Simon Pegg and starring Pegg and Nick Frost. The film follows a group of friends reattempting an "epic" pub crawl. The three have previously worked together on the television series *Spaced*, as well as the other two films in the so-called "Three Flavours Cornetto Trilogy", *Shaun of the Dead* (2004) and *Hot Fuzz* (2007).

The film is being produced by Big Talk Productions, StudioCanal and Working Title Films. Filming began in September 2012 at locations in Welwyn Garden City and Letchworth Garden City.. Part of the film was also shot at High Wycombe railway station in High Wycombe, Buckinghamshire.

The film is scheduled to be released in the United Kingdom on 14 August 2013 and in the United States on 25 October 2013.

Plot

Five childhood friends reunite after twenty years to repeat a legendary pub crawl from their youth, returning to their hometown once again to attempt to reach the fabled pub "The World's End". Over the course of the night, they begin to realise that the real struggle is "not just theirs but humankind's", and completing the crawl becomes the least of their worries.

Wright has described the film as an example of the social science-fiction genre, in the tradition of John Wyndham and Samuel Youd.

Cast

Simon Pegg as Gary King
Nick Frost as Andy Knight
Rosamund Pike
Paddy Considine
Martin Freeman
Eddie Marsan
Zak Bailess
Source http://en.wikipedia.org/wiki/The_World's_End